1001 WONDERFUL WONDERS

ACTIVITIES FOR *ALL* CHILDREN

ANNE ROGOVIN

Abingdon Press
Nashville

1001 Wonderful Wonders: Activities for *ALL* Children

Copyright © 1992 by Anne Rogovin

All rights reserved.

This book is printed on recycled, acid-free paper.

Library of Congress Cataloging-in-Publication Data

Rogovin, Anne.
   1001 wonderful wonders : activities for all children / Anne
Rogovin.
      p.   cm.
   ISBN 0-687-29193-3 (alk. paper)
   1. Creative activities and seat work.   I. Title.   II. Title: One thousand one
wonderful wonders.   III. Title: One thousand and one wonderful wonders.
LB1027.25.R64   1992   92-22882
372.5—dc20   CIP

MANUFACTURED IN THE UNITED STATES OF AMERICA

To

My parents who taught me a little of compassion

My best friend and husband, Milton, whose life is
dedicated to the betterment of humankind

Our children Ellen, Mark (his wife, Carolyn), and Paula
(her husband, Peter), whose lives also are dedicated
to the betterment of humankind

Our grandchildren (David, Malaika, Steven, Aliya,
and Eric), whose lives (we hope) will also be dedicated
to the betterment of humankind

ACKNOWLEDGMENTS

My deep appreciation goes to:

Edward Asner (and his little Charlie), a beautiful human being, the Salt of the Earth—who believes in *1001 Wonderful Wonders* and wrote the foreword.

All those who took the time from their busy lives to say such kind words for it.

Susan Heidorf Poole (Community Relations Coordinator for People, Inc.), who generously volunteered and worked so diligently to put all the "wonders" on the computer. Also, Kira Heidorf, who worked along with Susan until she had to leave Buffalo.

Aliya and Malaika Hart, our granddaughters, who contributed poetry. Also, their mother Ellen, an inner-city teacher in Philadelphia for twenty-six years (as is Paula in New York City for nineteen years). Each of our children gave lots of suggestions and criticism, especially Mark, an artist, and Carolyn, past director of the Sierra Club of Illinois.

CONTENTS

FOREWORD

The other day I was watching television with my four-year-old son, Charlie. As he flipped through the channels, I couldn't help being amazed by the way he seemed to watch for a moment, take in the flashing images and sounds and then move on, as if certain that the next channel would have what he was searching for. I began to wonder, in this fast-paced, media-oriented world, do our children ever get a chance to observe the world at their own pace or are they forced to speed up and adapt themselves to an adult pace?

A short while later, my question was answered. As we were walking down the street, Charlie kept stopping to look at things—leaves, sticks, birds. Other times, he would pause to listen—a lawn mower, a fire engine. Each new thing provoked a new question, a new observation. In responding to his questions I soon found myself observing the world around me in ways that I had never considered before. And above all else, I realized that, in some ways, children are the most adaptable people of all. And why not? Everything in the world is to them a new discovery, a wonder to be amazed at.

Unfortunately, as adults we often lose our sense of wonder and from time to time may need a little reminder. My suggestion: Take a walk with a child in one hand and *1001 Wonderful Wonders* in the other, and see and hear and feel what a wonderful feeling it is to experience the world through the eyes of a child.

—Edward Asner

INTRODUCTION

All parents want their children to grow to be healthy, happy, and productive adults. It wasn't always easy to accomplish this in the past. Nowadays it may be even more difficult. I am concerned about excessive television watching, absorption with computer games, and, the materialism that seems to bombard our childrens' waking hours. These make the parents' objective much harder to achieve successfully.

I am concerned about the well-meaning parents who pressure their children very early—at two, three, four, and five years of age. We all know ambitious parents who want their child to get into the "best" classes in preparation to getting into the "best" colleges. The young child is battered with so much information—as if the child were a reservoir to be filled with water, that the more water that flows into every nook and cranny, the more the child will be "educated."

I am concerned that the critical experience of having uninterrupted time for a child will pass, never to be replaced and never to bear the fruit it should. A child needs so many, many precious experiences to

delight	explore
pretend	make choices
make mistakes	plan
experiment	daydream (yes!)

and explore the wonderful world we live in through the five wonderful senses.

It is my hope that your child will find these "wonders" simple, uncomplicated, and "ordinary." I refer to such things as playing with pots and pans, sorting knives, forks, and spoons, or just picking up a leaf and looking at it.

It is my hope that though many of the "wonders" may not be new to us adults—they will nevertheless be fresh to a child. To the child, it doesn't make any difference at all if millions of children through time immemorial have floated leaves in rain puddles or stuffed acorns in pockets!

It is my hope that your child will be given a wide variety of experiences, "wonders." Not only will the child enjoy them, research studies show over and over again that a wide variety of experiences enrich and broaden a child's horizons. Children gain more than we realize from a hike in the woods, a visit to the zoo, or attending a concert in the park.

It is my hope that your child will be given responsibilities in the home as soon as possible. Even at three, there are small chores—in the kitchen, in the playroom, outdoors—a child can do. In fact, a child may even consider this "grown-up" and "fun" (yes! if it's handled the right way). In a way, when you think about it, a child who doesn't have work to do may be considered a deprived child.

It is my hope that none of the "wonders" is considered a game just to amuse the child (although it may well be lots of fun for the child). Or that "wonders" are presented to "educate" the child (although it might well do this too). My hope is that the child will get the critical mental habit of experiencing the world and become wiser and enriched by it.

It is my hope that a child is given time to spend with the parent or parents. How important this is to the child—even five minutes of cuddling, sometimes just to sit quietly with the parent or to talk while the parents listen, perhaps to take a short walk around the block together, exchanging ideas, being silly, singing out loud—or looking at the changing colors of the tree leaves. The sense of importance this gives the child cannot be measured.

It is also my hope that your child will get from *1001 Wonderful Wonders* a love for the natural world of our planet. And yet love is not enough. I hope that my little book will give the child a feeling that our earth is a sacred trust here for us to use, but to use well, to preserve and protect and leave in good condition for others.

Rachel Carson sums up my feelings so succinctly: "If a child is to keep alive his inborn sense of wonder . . . he needs the companionship of at least one adult who can share it, rediscovering with him the joy, excitement, and mystery of the world we live in."

NATURE WONDERS

*Nature is ever our companion, whether we will it or not. Even though we
are determined to shut ourselves in offices, nature sends her messengers.
The light, the moon, the clouds, the rain, the wind, the falling star,
the fly, the bouquet, the bird, the cockroach—they are all ours.
If one is to be happy, he must be in sympathy with common things.
He must live in harmony with his environment.
One cannot be happy yonder nor tomorrow;
he is happy here and now, or never.
Our stock of knowledge of common things should be great.
Few of us can travel.
We must know the things at home.*

—The Nature Study Idea, L. H. Bailey

1. Are you like an open-mouthed little baby bird that gobbles
up anything the mother or father offers? Your food is
everywhere:

at home	in an elevator	in a plane
at the seashore	at the zoo	in a cornfield
in the bakery	in a cave	on a riverbank
in the woods	in a desert	at a beauty parlor
in the kitchen	on a ranch	at the playground
in the snow	in a lighthouse	at a picnic
in a store	at the post office	at a pickle factory
in an apple orchard	on a train	on the front porch
in the grocery store		

even on a mountaintop!

2. Look carefully at Queen Anne's Lace and see its marvelous
construction!

3. Think about this . . .
The tallest tree started from one tiny seed.

4. Think about all the wonderful things just one tree can do:

The leaves can whisper in the breeze for a whole summer.
The leaves can crackle in the fall.
A pile of leaves can be jumped on.
You can pick an apple and eat it.
Do you like maple syrup?
A squirrel can run up a tree when a dog is chasing it.
You can swing from a tree.
When it's hot out you can take a nap under a tree, or just sit or eat under it.
You can climb a tree and look out.

5. Do you know what it would be like if there were no insects? We might not get any mosquito bites or bee stings—but do you know that lots of birds and other animals and fish would die without the insects for food?

6. Did you ever see a flock of migrating birds?
Did you ever wonder where they're coming from and where they're going?

7. See if you can keep your eyes off a duck family with little ducklings neatly in a line behind their mother.

8. No one who really loves nature would crush snails, an earthworm, a daddy longlegs—or most insects. Would you?

9. When you find ant nests, you're really lucky! But you must be sure not to disturb them! Just look.

See the different sizes and colors of the ants.

What are the ants carrying to their nests? Do you see two carrying the same load?

If a procession of ants is carrying food to their nest, do they follow the same route coming and going?

What are they carrying? any worms? bread crumbs?

Do you see any ants with wings? (They're the king and queen ants.)

Are any ants fighting?

Are any ants working on a tunnel?

(If you want a free and exciting show in your home, scoop up some ants in a jar with some tiny holes punched in the lid. Add some earth and leaves. Watch them for a few days. Then dump them in the garden so they can be free once again.)

10. Did you ever see the moon when it looked like a great big ball? when it looked like half of a ball? a skinny slice of melon?

11. A woodpecker has a sharp bill so it can peck trees and get out the insects.

Do you know that the pelican has a very large bill for scooping up fish to eat?

Did you ever see the hummingbird's bill and see how it sucks the nectar from flowers?

12. Hang a pile of left-over yarn, old thread, ribbon, and small pieces of cloth on a tree branch so the birds can use it to build a house.

Did you ever accidentally spot on a bird's nest the same piece of red yarn you once hung on the branch?

13. Did a mushroom ever pop up overnight on your lawn? Take a good look at it.

14. If you are ever lucky enough to catch a daddy longlegs, one of the funniest things to watch is daddy cleaning his legs. He is also a very good runner because his legs are so big.

(Incidentally, if he should ever lose a leg, don't feel sorry for him, because he can grow a new one. Yes!)

15. Have you ever thought about plants and wondered if it would be possible for anything to live on earth without them?

Let's see:

A hamburger comes from a steer. The steer can't live without grass (a plant).

What about bread? It is made from a plant (wheat).

What about eggs? They come from an animal that needs plants for food.

What about sugar? That was a plant (sugar cane).

Honey? Honey would not be made if bees could not get pollen from plants.

We could trace back any food this way. It all comes down to this: No plants—No life. Isn't that an interesting thing to think about?

16. Do you think you would ever want to change these things? Don't you think you will always love:

the exciting changes of the seasons that come step by step, year by year?

the same wildflowers?

cardinals, robins, beetles?

thistle?

maple trees?

tulips and violets?

to hear the bumblebees?

Wouldn't you want to find these same old beautiful things every morning?

17. If for no other reason at all, try to have a gerbil for a pet to see the funny things it will do. Such as:

crawl up your arm or
hide in your pocket

See how it bustles around old socks, paper, bells, empty toilet paper rolls—anything!

18. Who will be the first one in your family to find the first robin in spring? Will it be you?

19. Did you ever stop to think of all the different kinds of walks you can take? There is hardly any kind of walk you can't take.
Here are some:

winter walks	tree walks	a with-your-mom-
nighttime walks	snow walks	or-dad walk
morning walks	fall walks	a with-your-sister-
afternoon walks	sunrise walks	or-brother walk
sleet walks	spring walks	walks with your
hail walks	rain walks	friends
bird walks	summer walks	or maybe, just a walk
flower walks	insect walks	with your dog!

20. Because frogs are the same color as plants, it's pretty hard to find one. But have you ever heard a frog croak? Will that help you find one?

21. What a wonderful, wonderful thing just a little brook is . . .

Minnows play in it.
The sun kisses it.

Plants grow in it.
Grass grows on its banks.
It ripples in the wind.
It makes you want to follow it as it goes on and on.
A brook is just right for children.

22. Nighttime is usually sleeping time—isn't it? But some clear winter evening what an adventure it would be to stay up a bit later, take a walk to a nearby open space, and just look up at the starry sky.

(Of course, watching from the window or from a porch can be an adventure too!)

23. Was there a snowfall last night? Go outdoors before the walkers and shovelers, and look for animal tracks. Do you find dog tracks? squirrel tracks? mouse tracks? Follow them to see where they went.

24. Lie on your back and just watch the clouds. Are they heavy and black? Do any look like an animal you know? Are they moving fast? Do you think there'll be a rainstorm?

25. When you stop to think about it, seeds are a pretty wonderful part of a plant. For example:

Rice is a seed and a great number of the people of the world eat rice as their main food!
We eat wheat, corn, barley, and oat seeds.
We even get oils from seeds, like corn oil, cottonseed oil, peanut oil, and sunflower oil!

26. One of the showiest and sweetest smelling trees is the magnolia. If one is blooming, please try to smell it.

27. Plant a sunflower seed and watch it grow (It probably will grow taller than you, your big brother, or your father!)

28. If your pet turtle or guppy died, would you flush it down the toilet or throw it out in the garbage can? Or would you show how much you really loved it and bury it carefully in your backyard?

29. See the work that wind does by dangling a piece of cloth outside a window. Watch what it does on a windy day and then watch it on a still day. What does wind do to leaves?

30. Do you know that every green leaf of every plant is a factory to make food for the plant?

31. A leaf notebook helps build an awareness of the different colors and shapes of the leaves that are all around. (Look at the veins too so you see how the leaves are fed.)

32. Watch for the spider's artwork wherever you go—in gardens, garages, and (yes!) in houses too.

Did you ever look out at the grass on a sunny morning and see the threads of silk stretching from one grass stalk to another and how the web gleams with beauty?

Try to watch the great artist spin a web. (How it sparkles in the dew!)

If you're especially lucky, you may even glimpse the spider's supper caught in it!

33. Do you know that "weeds" have flowers too?

34. You would be surprised at all the birds there are on cold winter days (not all of them fly south).

> Just tie strips of fat around the branch of the tree in your yard and see them flocking to the feast!

35. The best thing you can do with an "orphaned" bird is to leave it alone. Usually, the parents are nearby. (If the bird is injured, be sure to have your parents call an animal-care center.)

36. What are some things that grow on you?

> your hair?
> your nails?

> Do you grow? Look at your baby picture. Put a tape mark on the door to show how tall you are. Look at the mark next year!

37. You'll be delightfully surprised when you dig down under some snow and bring up a shovelful of earth. Bring the earth indoors, and when it warms up a bit, see all the insects that were living there for the winter! (You will see them better if you use a magnifying glass.)

38. Is there an old sheet you can use? Place it under a bush and shake the bush. Watch its residents fall onto the sheet and then scurry off to freedom.

39. Did you ever see a sunrise? a sunset?

40. Did you ever see one or two loons sailing majestically up and down a lake and then suddenly dive out of sight for so long you thought they were sunk? And did they re-appear with their throats swollen from swallowing a fish?

41. Have you ever noticed that the different places you walk have different flowers growing in them? For example:

If you walk in the woods, look for trillium and hepaticas.

If you walk in the sunny fields, look for daisies and buttercups.

If you walk near a swamp, look for cattails.

If you walk near a pond, look for water lilies floating about.

42. Isn't it exciting to watch new puppies being born?
How many puppies are there?
What colors are they?
How are they getting their food?
Wouldn't you love to pick one up gently and cuddle it?

43. Be an "animal detective" when you go for a ride in the car in the city or the country. Can you spot any of these animals:

a deer	woodchucks	squirrels
cats	dogs	moose
a goat	horses	

44. Is there an out-of-the-way spot in your garden? Pile up grass cuttings, leaves, branches, dead flowers, etc., as a castle for insects to live in.

45. We all know that the automobile is very popular and important for people. But do you know that the automobile would probably not be as popular as it is if it weren't for trees?

Yes! When early cars were built, the tires were made

from natural rubber, which comes from the juice of certain trees!

46. Have you ever caught yourself looking up from what you were doing and just gazing at a plant for a couple of minutes?

47. A small, sunny patch in your backyard is all you need for your very own garden.

   If there is no space or if the space is not sunny, try planting in a plastic tub and putting it in the sun wherever you can find some. (Tomatoes, squash, zinnias, marigolds, geraniums—as well as string beans and peas—grow very well in a tub!)

   Then if you want the neighbors to admire your garden, all you have to do is move the tub to your front stoop!

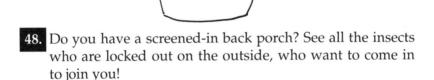

48. Do you have a screened-in back porch? See all the insects who are locked out on the outside, who want to come in to join you!

49. Besides petting and loving, find out these interesting things about your pet dog:

   his paws and what they look like
   his nose (whether it is hot or cold)
   his fur (the color or colors and what's underneath it)
   his teeth (Will he let you see them? Can you count them?)
   how he runs
   how he plays

how he eats (Does he chew his food or just gulp it down? What's his favorite food?)
how he sleeps (Does he like to curl up?)
where he likes to sleep best of all . . .

Do you know how old your dog is?

50. If there's a fly in your house, don't let anyone kill it!
See if you can get it inside a drinking glass that is upside down. (You'll need someone's help for this.)
See how wonderfully the fly is made—look at its wings; its legs; its eyes.
After a while, open the window or door so it will fly away.

51. Next time you go to the park, check to see if there is just the right size hill you can roll down.
Also see if the park has a cave you can explore. (Take an adult along.)

52. How close to a bird can you creep before it flies away?

53. Have you ever watched whirling red, yellow, and purple leaves dance to the ground?

54. Try this. Take a handful of soil from different places (such as your garden, the woods, or the park) and put each handful in a different container. Keep the soil moist and watch for the sprouts of the mysterious seeds hidden there.

55. Do you know that a spider in a tin can—or some ants in a jar—can make for a very special zoo to keep in your bedroom?

56. Have you ever seen a nut that is big, and so hard that it has to be opened with a hammer? But when it is opened, you find treasures like:

> delicious sweet coconut milk
> coconut meat, which can be chipped for making coconut cookies or put on your cereal.

57. When you see a honeybee on an apple blossom, think of what a wonderful apple can come from this visit.

58. Nature is pretty wonderful, isn't she?
To think that, with all the billions of people there are in the world and with all the billions of trees there are, no two are exactly alike!

59. Do you know that this very page, the one you are looking at, comes from a plant?

60. The cockroach may be a terrible nuisance, but he is really a very interesting fellow. If you should be able to catch one, put the prisoner in a vial with bread crumbs. Then watch him run like a streak when you release him outdoors.

61. When you go to the park, try never to forget to bring some bread crumbs for the ducks!

62. How long can you keep a milkweed seed in the air by blowing it?
(No hands allowed!)

63. Stand back and watch a bumblebee "bumble" around a flower to get the nectar.

Don't worry, she won't hurt you unless you bother her first!

64. A room that is teeming with the life of plants, birds, insects, and animals is the most beautiful room in the world!

65. Trees aren't just for woodlands. They are for:

city parks
apartment house grounds
shopping centers
parking lots
areas along curbstones

Can you think of any other places where we all need their help and beauty?

66. Isn't it interesting and wonderful to know of all the different parts of plants that we eat. For example:

When we eat asparagus and celery, we are eating stems.
When we eat beans, corn, and rice, we are eating seeds.
When we eat beets, carrots, radishes, and potatoes, we are eating roots.
When we eat lettuce and spinach, we are eating leaves.
When we eat broccoli, we are eating flower buds.
When we eat bananas—what are we eating?

67. Look at a dandelion seed. Then blow on it and see the wind carry the parachute away.

68. Cut off a piece of potato that has an "eye" on it and plant it in a pot of soil.
OR
Rest half a potato in water and watch how the roots grow down and the leaves climb up!

69. You don't have to be very old to get a lesson in soil erosion. Just let the garden hose squirt on some earth for a little while and see how the water digs into the earth.

70. Imagine a tiny pill that looks as if it were cut in half.
It could be all red or all red with black spots.
It could be all black or all black with red spots.
This pill is so clever, if you bother her even a little bit, she will just fold up her legs and act as if she were dead.
That little insect is a *ladybug*. She will not hurt you. If she lands on your arm, make up a little song to sing to her—or sing a song you already know:

"Lady bird, lady bird,
    fly away home.
Your house is on fire,
    your children all gone."

71. Did you ever see a bird make a mad dash into a hole in the trunk of a tree and wonder, "Now just what is going on inside there?"

72. To make a bouquet of dried flowers, gather flowers like goldenrod, thistle, or cattails into a clump and then hang them upside down to dry for about a week.
Then put them in a container in the kitchen for everyone to enjoy.

73. It isn't easy to find bird nests in the summertime because of all the leaves on the trees. But in the winter, when most of the trees are bare, look up at the branches and see if some round clumps are clinging to them!

74. Have you ever seen these signs of spring:

crocus?	dandelions?	pussy willows?
wet earth?	ants appearing?	frogs calling?
turtles bathing in the sun?	honeybees?	a ladybug?

a woodchuck when he gets up after sleeping all winter?

75. Plants are pretty wonderful.

They don't care who you are.
They don't care what you do.
They don't talk back.
They don't do anything bad.
They're just there for you to love and admire.

76. Have you ever wondered why birds sing?
Is it because they have things to discuss with one another?
Do they tell about the food that might be nearby?
Is it because they may want to warn one another of some danger?
Do you think they may want to attract a mate?
Of course, there may be some who just like to hear themselves sing!

77. Do you know why—on a cold winter's day—a bird has its head pulled in and its feathers are all fluffed up?

78. Someone will be very pleased if you put a pretty leaf or flower in the knothole of a wooden fence.

79. Have you ever watched a mother sparrow teaching her babies to fly?

80. All the wonderful ways nature has for her seeds to get about:

> Blow on a dandelion or milkweed to see their seeds float away on parachutes.
>
> Helicopters are easy. Toss maple or elm seeds in the air and see how they come down.
>
> Touch the slingshot pods of jewelweed.
>
> Tumbleweed seeds are tossed out of the old tumbleweed by the wind.
>
> Coconut seeds float like boats.
>
> What do squirrels do with their nuts and acorns?
>
> Eat an apple, throw out the core, and guess what could happen someday?
>
> If you stick a burr onto your sock, walk around awhile and then look down. You will see how the burrs of the burdock plant are hitchhikers!

81. Some lazy day when you feel like doing nothing but stretching out on your stomach on the grass, take a peek at what's living there.

> Do you see any ants? any worms? spiders? grasshoppers?
>
> If you should see a caterpillar, let it climb from your hand all the way up your arm.

82. Did you ever listen to the cooing of a pigeon? What do you think it might be saying?

83. The song of the katydid often lasts all night long. Listen:

> "Katy-did, she didn't, she did!"
>
> The katydid looks like a grasshopper. Find one and keep it in a vial for a while. Then let it fly home.

84. You may be able to see a whole "forest" if you eat your breakfast near the kitchen window. See the:

gnarled trees   pine trees   a monarch butterfly
willow, maple,   cocoons   clumps of bushes
   and oak trees   cats
a furry striped chipmunk climbing around the trees like a squirrel!

85. Find a leaf you like a lot. Do you like its color? its shape? Put it in a glass of water so you can enjoy it for a long time.

86. When you see the oriole's nest, which looks like a pocket dangling from the limb of a tree, do you think it was built this way to get a free ride when the breezes blow?

87. a coffee can

a small, narrow jar or bottle   a test tube
a cheese or margarine container   a salt shaker
an empty cologne bottle   a frozen juice container

Any one of these containers is just right to hold a fistful of buttercups for a Mother's Day present!

88. When you see a violet living in the woods, you can see what William Wordsworth meant by his song:

"A violet by a mossy stone
Half hidden from the eye!
—Fair as a star, when only one
Is shining in the sky."

89. Once you start loving stones, you may never stop keeping your eyes open for them. Can you find any that are:

smooth?   gritty?

rough?	glassy?
grainy?	scratchy or sparkly?
round or square?	thin or fat?

90. Is there a soft misty shower? Put on your raincoat for a little walk and see the rain-washed world. After the shower, is there a rainbow?

91. When you go for a walk, keep your eyes open for animal homes. Do you see any:

bird nests in trees?
hives (houses for bees)?
burrows (holes in the earth for rabbits)?
webs (spun webs in which a caterpillar can live)?
ant hills (mounds built by ants)?

92. Besides enjoying animals as pets, can you think of other ways we are glad there are animals? What do they give us?

meat to eat
wool for sweaters and blankets
milk for grown-ups and children to drink
help in carrying heavy loads

Have you ever seen a "seeing eye" dog help blind people? What else can you think of?

93. Always try to keep your eyes open when you are outdoors. You never know what you'll find:

a bird feather to add to your collection
a lawn full of dandelions that hasn't been mowed yet
tiny tracks of birds
a tumbleweed tumbling along in the wind
an apple tree in blossom
a busy ant to follow

94. When you see a bird on the ground, notice that some hop,

a robin bounces along,
a starling walks,
a blackbird just strolls,
     and
a morning dove waddles!

95. See what happens when one plant sits on a windowsill and another one sits in a dark corner. Try this out for a week.

96. Have you ever seen the day begin? Does the dark sky start to look brighter and then get pinkish, reddish, and golden?

97. Do you have a pet cat?
How does she drink her milk?
How does she eat? sleep?
What makes her purr?
How many whiskers does she have?

98. One of the most truly wonderful things in the world to watch is how a funny-looking caterpillar changes into a beautiful butterfly.
See if you can help capture one in a milkweed and put it in a jar. Sprinkle the leaves with water and add other leaves every once in a while. Watch every day till a cocoon appears. Then
     wait
     and wait
     and wait.
It will be really worthwhile waiting when you see the truly marvelous change happen . . . a beautiful butterfly! Admire her for a while. Then you'll let her flutter off, won't you?
She has a lot of work to do!

99. You really don't need much money to buy a goldfish house. Just a bowl of water and some food from the pet shop are all you need to house and feed your new friend.

100. Can you find or buy a turtle you can have for a pet?
Watch the turtle when it's frightened. See its head, legs, and tail all disappear into its shell.
When it feels safe, see its head and legs reappear outside the shell!

101. So you think wildlife is only in the country and in the woods! How wrong you are! If you are very quiet and stealthy you can find:

a house mouse
seagulls, pigeons, robins
centipedes and millipedes
spiders, cockroaches, and fleas
bats in attics
muskrats in city parks
deer near the edge of cities
and skunks EVERYWHERE!

Have you ever watched a raccoon raid a garbage can?

102. A bag should always be in your pocket for bringing home things you find, like:

a pretty leaf
a colorful stone
OR
a dead beetle!

103. Is there a dandelion growing in your garden? Put it in a glass of water and place it by the windowsill.

104. Don't you think it's understandable why ants like stones so much? Who wouldn't—if you could go under a stone to cool off from a hot summer sun or stay warm at night!
And besides, it's such a cozy nursery for having babies.

105. Toward the end of winter, bring in some branches of the pussy willow, forsythia, and other bushes and put them in a jar of water.
Then watch what happens.

106. Did you ever hear a cat yowl in the middle of the night? Did you ever wonder why she yowls?

107. An empty tuna can with some earth and a seed (or small plant that has a root on it) makes a present fit for a king, or a queen!

108. Have you ever seen a log-and-stick dam that was made by a beaver?

109. Everyone should really admire a snail. Just imagine carrying your home with you and going inside when you're scared. Watch the snail climb over obstacles or hang from a ceiling. See how it will climb on just about anything with just one foot! Put a snail on its back and see what happens!

110. Is there a crack in your sidewalk?
Look carefully.
Is something growing in it?

111. When you stop to think about it—
every earthworm is doing something wonderful for the garden.

Every mantis feeding on another insect is doing something for the garden.

Every bee that visits the flowers is on an errand for the garden as well as for itself.

112. There are enough kinds of gardens to please just about every person in the world. Here are some to consider:

the usual row gardens with lettuce, tomatoes, carrots, and so on

a sunflower jungle for birds

a salad garden, just of salad greens like lettuce and endive

an Italian garden with tomatoes, eggplant, green peppers

a Chinese garden including chinese celery and snow peas

a giant garden with just pumpkins and watermelons

Some people have gardens that are just for butterflies and bees, like zinnias and marigolds.

Some people have gardens of just perennials, like bleeding heart and sedum.

Some might want a garden that is just for color.

Some might want a garden of nothing but different varieties of fern.

Some want a garden that is very formal.

Some prefer a garden that is in the style of faraway places.

And someone might just have a garden in a dish in the windowsill.

Which would you like to have now? someday?

EXPLORATION WONDERS

I AM A GIRL WHO DREAMS

I am a girl who dreams.
I wonder what it's like
To fly free like a bird.
I dream of being an eagle
With wings as big as the sun
I hope someday I can reach
For the sun, sky, and clouds;
Flying higher and higher.
No one knows where I'm going
And where I've been
I am a girl who dreams
Of being an eagle.

—*Aliya Hart*

113. It's really very worthwhile to take a trip to any part of the neighborhood to watch a paved street being ripped up for repaving!

114. Have you ever been to any of these terminals:
a bus terminal?
a railroad terminal?
an airline terminal?

115. Is that new bridge (or highway) finally finished? Are they having a dedication? Even if you don't understand all that they are saying, you may enjoy seeing all the people there and also looking down from the bridge.

116. Did you ever ride on an elevator—one with an elevator operator or one with buttons to press?

Did you ever ride on an escalator?
Which do you like better—an elevator or an escalator?
or
would you rather go up and down on steps?

117. If there is a dog show at your park, don't miss it! It's fun to see all the different dogs and watch how their masters prepare them for the dog "beauty" contest.

118. Who wouldn't *love* a visit to the zoo?

When you get there, say "Hi!" to the zebra.
When you see the kangaroo, does it make you want to hop too?
See the snapping turtle.
Does it look like all the animals are smiling at you?
Did you see the baby gorilla that was just born? a baboon reserve?
Did you feed the goats?
Will that pretty white rabbit let you hug it? (It seems to be there just for you to love.)
Did you ride in the air on a "skyfari"?
   or take a train ride
   or a monorail ride through the wilds of Africa?
What about a real camel ride, perched on a bump?
Why do all the animals keep smiling at you?
Did you get a box of popcorn?
   Are you tired?

119. When the family is out driving in the car and you come to a little town or village you've never been to before— why not go out and explore a bit.

Go down its main street and look at the stores and the people who live there.

Go down the side streets and see the houses. Are they
new or very, very old houses?

Does it have a little school where all the children go—
or do you think they may be bused to a large, central
school?

What work do the people who live here do? Do they
work as farmers or do they commute to the cities?

120. When your parents are having the car washed, sit by the
window of the car as it goes by the different machines—
and don't miss a thing that is happening!

121. Have you ever gone for a ride in a canoe? a rowboat? a
ferryboat? an oceanliner? a kayak?

Have you ever been on a river? a lake? a pond? a little
stream? an ocean?

122. Is there an old, old, old tree that you can go to see?
Hug it!

123. If you live in the city you will just love a visit to a farm.
Do you have a friend or relative who has a farm you can
visit?

See the fields of cabbages, onions, oats, and barley
stretched out for miles and miles.

Get a firsthand experience of the farmer plowing up
the earth with a tractor.

Will the farmer let you sit on the tractor seat?

See the farmer seeding the fields with the seeder.

See the mowing, reaping, and baling.

Watch the farmer milk the cows. Is it done "by hand"
or is a special milking machine used?

Does the farmer have a chicken coop? Do you see the
eggs being collected? Would you like to help a little?

Will the farmer let you pick some peas or tomatoes or apples? (Maybe the farmer will let you take some home!)

Does the farmer have a cider mill? (Maybe the farmer will let you see how cider is made. Maybe your parents will buy a gallon to take home!)

Is the farmer chopping wood for a fire?

Will the farmer let you slide down a *hayloft?*

(If—for whatever reason—you cannot go to a real farm, your local zoo could be the next best thing!)

124. Did you ever go inside a trailer or visit a trailer park?

125. A grown person may have seen grain elevators many times—but wouldn't you like to see some too? And wouldn't you like to go inside one of them to see what goes on there? Do they have a visiting day for families?

126. If you live in a crowded city, you might be fascinated by a visit to a garden nursery to see:

the huge variety of trees, shrubs, and flowers
little seedlings growing in the hot house

(A nursery is especially fun to visit before a holiday!)

127. Would you like to browse through a furniture store and pretend you are picking out furniture for a "dream house"? Or would you like to pick out the big bed you would like to have someday?

128. If there is a science museum in your town, it might have things you would enjoy:

special afternoon and Saturday classes for children
(classes on snakes, flowers, insects, etc.)
special nature movies for children
a live animal section
a stuffed animal section
a summer camping program on the museum grounds
a hiking or bird watching club?
Indian folk dancing classes for children
a shop where they sell nature books and gifts made
from things of nature (like cornhusk dolls, seed
beads, etc.)

Wouldn't it be nice if your parents joined the museum
and you could take part in some of these activities?

129. Ride through a state or national park. Do you see
camping areas? Would you like to go camping there
someday?

130. If you should ever—ever—come across a roadside sign
saying you will soon be coming to a special museum
that has old cars (or old trains, or carriages, or trolleys),
you must *stop* and visit it. How would you like to ride in
one of those carriages or old cars down your block?

131. Maybe someday you can visit some big estate with a
special garden, like a Japanese garden that is made of
just sand and rocks!

132. You can see pictures of baby animals in picture books,
but when you can have the firsthand experience of
touching a baby goat or a baby horse—that's something
you can never forget!

133. Is there a kite-flying meadow where you can go to fly
your kite or watch others fly their kites?

134. Do you think you could ever, ever be bored by watching the neighbors' house being painted?

135. Next time you and your parents go out for a drive, bring along a lunch so you can stop and eat near a beautiful waterfall.

136. Did you ever watch the steel frame for a building being assembled? Does it remind you a little of a human skeleton?

137. If you happen to live just east of the Rocky Mountains, you will enjoy driving through plains where the sky seems to go on forever. If you're there at sunset, you will be able to see the sun go all the way down to the ground.

138. Go to places where people:

sing	shape pottery	weave baskets
make jewelry	paint pictures	create sculptures
sew quilts	carve wood	knit or crochet
blow glass	sew dresses	play instruments

Would they let you watch them for a while?
Would you like to be able to do any of these things someday?

139. Is there a pickle cannery anywhere—*anywhere!*—around that you can visit?

140. Sometime when your parents and you have a little extra time, get on a bus and ride to the end of the line and then go back to where you started.

141. Visit an animal shelter and just see if you can leave without wanting to adopt a homeless cat or dog!

142. Would you like to go on a conducted tour through a big cave?

143. Wouldn't it be a real treat to be able to stay as long as you wanted to watch an old factory building being knocked down with a big bulldozer?

144. If you can, visit an area where there are locks. Be very patient, and if you wait long enough, you may see the locks lower or raise the water so boats can go through the gates.

145. Sometimes the lobby of a neighborhood bank has exhibits of art created by neighborhood artists or by children in a nearby school.
   Would you like to have some of your artwork there someday? Maybe you will!

146. If you are ever by a river or even just a tiny stream—enjoy its beauty—but think a tiny bit about:

   how rivers help our earth
   how they water the land so we can raise our food
   how they give drinks to birds and other animals
   how they are homes for fish and beavers
   how they move logs to lumberyards
   how they move our food to markets in the city

   And there are still more wonderful things they do!

147. Is there anyone who doesn't like to watch a parade? Have you ever watched:

a St. Patrick's Day parade?
a Hispanic Day parade?
a parade on Martin Luther King, Jr., Day?
a local church parade?
a local high school parade?
a Save-the-Earth parade?

Did you ever see a Peace parade? a parade for the
homeless?
Would you ever like to march in a parade?

148. Does your new neighbor happen to:

be of a color different from yours?
be of a religion different from yours?
speak a language different from yours?
wear clothing different from yours?

How *lucky* you are!
Can your parents invite the family over for a cook-out
in the backyard
or
invite the family over just to sit on your back porch
and talk together?
Do they have a young child who can be your new
friend?

149. Does your neighborhood park have:

a playground for children?
a swimming pool?
a wading pool for children?
a picnic area?
a lake or pond for canoeing, rowing, or fishing?

In winter, does the park allow ice-skating? tobogganing?
Are there any special free outdoor events like:

a "big" baseball game?
free outdoor plays?

free outdoor concerts?
ice carnivals?
puppet shows?
dog shows?

(Be sure to bring along a blanket to sit on.)

150. See if the corner store owner will let you "peek behind the counter" someday when he or she isn't too busy.

151. If you can visit a bakery, look at the gigantic ovens. Do they look like your oven at home? Notice how much they bake at one time!
   What kind of clothes do the bakers wear? Would you like to wear a baker's hat?
   Wouldn't you love to help put the icing on cakes!

152. Watch the sanitation trucks collect garbage on your street. (Do you admire the workers for the important work they do to keep your community clean?)

153. If there is time to see only one thing at the city aquarium, plan to visit the seals and just see if you can keep your eyes off their performance!

154. Look around—does your city have a beautiful skyline you can see? Watch it at twilight to see how it changes.

155. Do your parents have to buy some lumber? Go with them to the lumberyard and browse around. See the different kinds of wood.
   Watch how the wood is sawed. Will they let you have the shavings to take home?
   If the lumberyard has any scrap pieces of lumber, will they let you have some to take home to make building blocks for palaces, forts, and towers?

156. Someday when your parents have some extra time, just browse through a big shopping plaza.

Look at the window displays. Are there any big sales going on?

Go into the department stores. Will any have a fashion show you can watch?

Is someone demonstrating a new electrical appliance?

Are they demonstrating how to cook something new? Would you like to have a sample to taste?

Enjoy the holiday decorations.

Are there any senior citizens taking their daily walks for exercise?

When you're finished, will you be able to stop at the cozy restaurant there for a cold drink or a sandwich?

157. How many of these farms have you ever gone to:

a turkey farm?   a dairy farm?   a chicken farm?
a cattle farm?   a tree farm?   a tobacco farm?
a truck farm? (What is a truck farm?)

Wouldn't you love to go to an organic farm for fruits and vegetables?

158. Of course, cemeteries are mostly for people who have died, but they are also wonderful places just to walk around and look at the trees and birds. Sometimes there are little ponds or streams there.

159. See if a friendly butcher will let you visit his shop. Watch how he:

cuts the meat
grinds the meat to make hamburger
cuts the chicken into "parts"

Would he let you visit the refrigerator where meat is stored?

160. Have you ever taken a ride on a ferryboat?

161. Write ahead to a television station for permission to attend a televised children's show.

162. Take a "Let's-Do-It-Today" trip to the waterfront.

163. Did you ever see workers work at an "assembly line"? Check out the newspapers and see if any local assembly plant is having an "open house."

164. Look at the billboards on a walk or when you are in the car.
> Would you rather see the ones that try to sell cigarettes, fancy clothes, and perfumes
>> or
> would you rather see billboards that tell you about the local animal shelter, about planting trees, or about how to save the city orchestra?

165. Wouldn't it be thrilling to visit the places where your mother and father were born?
> Are their old houses still there? Do you think you could get permission to go inside?
> Can you visit the schools they went to?
> Where did they play when they were little?

166. Digging a ditch may be humdrum for most adults to watch—but for a child it's SPELLBINDING!

167. Is there a short train ride you can take that goes between two nearby stations?

168. No matter where you live, you can usually find a wooded lot to explore. (If you live in the city, you might find one just about at the edge of it.)

169. Next time your parent goes to the post office, see if he or she will be able to take a little extra time so you can see:

how people line up for their "turn"
how the clerks weigh the packages
how stamps are sold in big sheets and some in little books

Have you ever seen the twenty-nine cent "love" stamp?
any animal or bird stamps?
any stamps of famous people?

What picture is on the new Postal Service postcard?
Are there women as well as men working as clerks?

170. Stop at an outdoor flower market just to smell the flowers.

171. Large city airports are usually too big and too busy for a child to enjoy. A smaller airport usually has all the action in one building so you can see more easily:

the ticket sales window
the check-in counter
how baggage is handled
the planes loading and unloading passengers
and the planes landing and taking off!

Have you ever taken a plane ride? If you haven't, would you like to someday?

172. Have you ever visited an international food shop? See if you are able to go away empty-handed!

173. Do your parents know anyone who has a pigeon roost you can visit? Maybe the owner will let you hold a pigeon. Maybe he or she will tell you interesting stories about pigeons and how they can carry messages to faraway places and come all the way back again.

174. Did a sign in the road say you are coming near a pioneer log cabin? How lucky you are!
    Stop and look at it.
    Would you be allowed to go inside?
    Would you like to live in a log cabin?
    Maybe someday you will be able to visit a pioneer village that has lots of log cabins.

175. It's not a pleasant sight, but wouldn't it be interesting to see the injury to a tree struck by lightning? Don't you think so?

176. Is the street-sprinkler truck coming down your street? Watch how the machine sloshes the dirt away. (Do you help to keep your street nice and clean?)

177. Wouldn't you *love* to go to a corn festival?

178. If possible, visit houses of worship like:

    a cathedral   a church   a synagogue
    a mosque   a Hindu temple

Do you enjoy the songs they sing?

Do they have any paintings on their walls? any murals? statues? stained-glass windows? any other religious symbols?

179. Does your older brother or sister belong to a swimming club at school and is there a swimming meet you can attend?

180. Do you have a backyard fireplace where you can tell stories or just talk to one another—just you and the family?

or

you and your friend or friends?

or

you and the new little boy or girl and their parents who just moved in on your block?

181. Can your parents arrange a visit to a fire station?

Wouldn't it be great if you could sit in the fire engine on the driver's seat?

What do the firefighters do when they aren't putting out fires?

Do they eat at the fire station?

Do they sleep or rest there?

Do they clean the fire engines?

Could you try on a *firefighter's hat?*

182. It may take a day's ride, but maybe your parents will want to take the family to an "open house" at a famous fort.

183. You will want to return to a library over and over again—if there is a chance to:

get your own library card and pick out your own books to read

attend the weekly "story hour"

browse through the children's magazines
pick out a record or two to take home
see a special exhibit of foreign dolls or Native American crafts
see a marionette show

Are there any children's books about:

people who live in faraway places?
people who have different religions?
people who have different colors of skin?
famous women?
people who have disabilities?

184. Some tall office buildings have "observation towers" you can look out from. Can you go up to one?
Can you see about where you live?
Can you see the factory area?
Can you see the downtown shopping area? the cars in the streets?
Can you see all the people? Do they look like little ants?

185. There are street fairs held by all ethnic and immigrant groups—African American, Hispanic, Greek, Italian, Polish, Chinese, Native American, and so on. Try not to miss them—they're so much fun!

Listen to their music.
Eat their foods.
Watch their dances.
Maybe you'll hear some people speak different languages.
Are there any of them wearing "different" clothes?
Are there any mementoes you can buy so you will remember the fair for a long time?
Doesn't it make you proud and glad that so many different people make up our country?

186. When you go for a bus ride through a neighborhood that is new to you, try to sit near a window.

187. Next time your parents go to a gas station, get permission (if they're not in a big hurry) to watch what goes on there.
  Stand aside and watch gasoline being pumped into the gas tank.
  See how a tire is changed.
  How are the cars washed?
  How are cars raised so repairs can be made?
  What else do you see?

188. Stop a few minutes at the store that always has things of nature for its window displays. Things like:

  bouquets of real flowers held by mannequins
  posters and landscape paintings for backgrounds
  jewelry suspended from branches of trees
  pottery set on pretty stones or shells
  pinecones and acorns scattered about for the displays of fall clothing

189. Schoolyards are places for children to play. But you can also watch the older boys and girls play baseball, football, and soccer games.

190. If you live in the country, would you ever like to take a whirl in the city just to go window-shopping?

191. Have you ever visited a horse stable?
  Watch horses being trained. See them jump hurdles.
  What do horses eat?
  Are there different kinds of horses?
  Sometimes you can see a person riding a carriage drawn by a horse!
  Would you like to ride a horse someday?
  Would you like to attend a horse show?

192. Is there a children's Saturday movie matinee (one that isn't violent) that you can go to with your parents? Can you bring your new little neighbor with you?

193. When you're out driving in the country, be sure to stop at a roadside fruit-and-vegetable market.
Can you buy a bushel basket of apples for the family?
Is there freshly picked corn? any tomatoes? potatoes? pumpkins? Can you buy a pumpkin?

194. If you like fish, you'll be enchanted by the huge variety of fish at a city aquarium. Is there an aquarium you can visit?
If not, see if a nearby pet shop stocks fish.

195. If a new house is being built, try to watch it from the beginning when the foundation is laid all the way to the new family moving in.
Will your parents welcome them into the neighborhood with a big pot of soup? (It may take the new family some time to have their stove connected.)
Do they have any little children who may become your new friends?

196. Wouldn't it be fun to drive out with the family to see a livestock auction?

197. Have you ever browsed around a hardware store while your parents are picking out a tool?
See if someone is making up some screens and storm windows.
What else does the hardware store sell?

kitchen supplies?
garden supplies?
auto supplies?

Would you like to work in a hardware store someday?

198. You'll enjoy visiting a sheep ranch—especially when it's sheepshearing time!

199. When you go to the dry cleaners with a parent—

Smell the different smells there.
Watch the machine that is used for ironing.
How does the checkout clerk know which clothes are yours?

200. Have you ever visited the places your mom and dad work?
Do they work at desks? an assembly line? on a truck?
Did you meet any of their coworkers or their "boss"?
Where do they keep their coats? In lockers?
Do they punch a time clock?
If you happen to be there at lunchtime, could you eat in their cafeteria too?

201. Do you know what a nature preserve is?
It's a place left alone to be as it always was.

the meadows   streams
the woods   and the birds
ponds and springs

Do you think you would like to visit a nature preserve?

202. It's a real treat to visit a police station, especially if you can have your friendly neighborhood police officer be your guide!

203. If your Sunday school has a picnic, why not invite the children of another faith to attend—then maybe you can attend theirs one day.

204. Watching a school baseball, football, or soccer game in the schoolyard can be just as exciting as any "big league" game (like at Yankee Stadium).

205. When you go into a big public building such as the downtown city hall, what do they have at the entrance to greet you?

Did you ever see a big mural with all kinds of people of different races and the work they do in the community?

Would you like to see a mural showing peace and friendship for everyone in the world?

206. If you have never eaten at a fast-food restaurant, see if you can someday. How different is it from eating at home or from a regular restaurant?

Do you like the self-service idea? Watch how orders are taken and how quickly they are filled.

Is there a jukebox playing?

Would you ever want to work in a fast-food restaurant?

207. Ask your mail carrier if you can meet him or her at the pick-up box near you and help deliver the mail on your block.

208. Have you ever seen maple trees being tapped? If you ever have an opportunity to go "sugaring off," don't pass it up!

(Maybe you could bring home some maple syrup for Sunday morning pancakes!)

209. If you live in a small community where most of the people are the same color, are of the same religion, come from the same country, and do the same work, you'll really enjoy a trip to a big city where things are quite different—*except* that they are all people who

laugh	cry
sing	get mad

like children, books, nature, flowers and trees, and
   more
                    just like you!

210. Do you know anyone who doesn't like bagels? Wouldn't it be fun to see how they are made—and then eat one when you're done!

211. Did you ever come across a tumbled mass of shells that was washed in from faraway?

212. A pet shop is a good place to watch animals. Most pet shopkeepers like children and will let you come in just to look.
   If you're especially lucky you may hear a talking bird
                    or
   see a batch of new puppies. (Maybe you will be allowed to buy one someday.)

213. Do you think you would enjoy visiting a fish hatchery? a fish cannery?

214. A nature preserve is a special swatch of land where nature is kept wild, a special place where they try to save rare plants like the pygmy plant, or where they want to save rare animals. Does your community have one you can visit?

215. Does your park have trails you can follow? Not only will the markers tell you which way to go, but there may be some very special surprises for you to see on the way!

216. If your parents should ever hear of a place where there is a corn tassel demonstration—do try to go there. You will enjoy seeing all the beautiful things you can make with the corn tassels. Maybe they will show you how to make a corn doll!

217. When you drive past a cornfield—go slowly to admire their beauty and think about the hard work that went into growing the cornstalks.

218. Did you ever see a silo sticking straight up in the air like a big office tower?
   What is a silo for? Can you get permission to go inside an empty one?

219. When you're driving in the country, stop the car when you see wheat rippling in the breeze.

220. Did you know that there are special "deer parks" where deer are protected from hunters and are safe to roam around?
   (Don't you wish there were special "monkey parks"?)

221. When you go to the center of a city—or a big shopping plaza, or an entrance to a big public building like the city art gallery—have you ever seen a big water fountain?

Stay there and enjoy it. If it happens to have some goldfish swimming in it, that makes it even more enjoyable—doesn't it?

222. There aren't many cities and towns that still have the old, old trolley cars. But if you should ever come across them in your family travels, do try to take a ride in one! (You'll never forget it!)

223. Try to find out if the cheese factory has a "Visitors' Day." It's a fascinating experience to see how gallons and gallons of milk are transformed into cheese!

224. It's quite possible that your parents may enjoy a guided tour through a candy factory as much as you (especially if they give everyone a sample of "you-know-what" at the end of it!).

SENSORY WONDERS

VISION

I sit in solitude
and my spirit is lifted
by the wings of the
dusky air. Columbines
cascade beside me
and wind dances
through the trees
pausing only slightly
to take breath.
As mountain streams
glisten, harmoniously
they compose the
pure, sweet song
heard not by ears
but felt by hearts;
the trees sway
with the rhythm.
Peacefulness, completeness.
Euphoria becomes me
and I become one
with the earth as
grasses lie under a
honey-covered blanket
and the goldenness
of being returns and
everything is touched
by the gentle kiss
of the sun's farewell.

—Malaika Hart

SEEING

225. When you look out at a sunset—don't hurry. Stay awhile and see how the colors change.

226. Have you ever seen a tree with a twisted shape?
Did you ever see a tree silhouetted against the sky?
When you look at it in wintertime, do the branches look like lace?

227. Have you looked at the sky today?

228. Is there some construction going on in your neighborhood? Stop and watch:

cranes lifting loads high into the sky
bulldozers crushing old foundations
swirling cement mixers
gigantic trucks carrying earth and rocks away

229. Look in the mirror. What is the color of your eyes?
What is the color of your hair?
Is your face clean or dirty?
Is your hair neat or messy?
Draw your face, looking at the mirror.

What do you look like when you drink a glass of water?
eat a carrot?
chew gum?

230. If you live in the country, a trip to the city is full of wonders to see, like:

traffic jams   museums and art galleries
skyscrapers   churches, cathedrals, synagogues

If you live in the city, a trip to the country could bring "firsts" like:

a farmer   fields of wheat, apple
a windmill   cows in a pasture   orchards
a rooster   a stream running
                     through a field

231. Notice how water-laden flowers drip in a rainstorm.

232. If these dried beans were mixed together, could you sort them out?

> black beans
> black-eyed peas
> chick peas or garbanzo
> kidney beans
> lima beans
> lentils
> green peas (whole and split)

233. Take a look around your neighborhood. Do you see:

> someone repairing a car?
> someone washing windows?
> people watering lawns?
> people sitting on porches?
> freshly cut grass?
> a baby in a playpen?
> the mail carrier stopping to say "hello" to someone?
> a house for sale?
> lots of cars?
> a dog running after a cat?
> anyone jogging?

234. The second best thing you can do if you can't go out in the rain is to sit on the porch and watch rain come down.

235. Just a short walk and look around can tell you so much about the wonderful, beautiful world we live in. How much there is to see! Look for:

> streams
> tall groves of trees
> rolling hills
> lake shores
> birds
> insects

mountains   country roads
stones   May flowers
people   and all kinds of weather
spider webs

236. Did you ever stop to watch the wind blowing a paper cup? Where did it land?

237. Visit a harbor to see: ocean liners
                          freighters
                          fishing boats
                          sailboats
                          rowboats
                          tugboats

238. If you're not allowed to go outdoors because the weather is bad or you're not feeling well, you can still enjoy yourself by looking out the window to see:

winds blowing leaves
black storm clouds
a sunrise that bursts into the world
a lingering sunset
the night studded with stars
people scurrying to get home from work

239. Just by looking out the window, can you tell if it's a windy day?
Is dust swirling around?
Are branches of trees swaying?
Is a flag waving wildly?
Have the clothes on the clothesline been blowing?

240. Look up at the clouds:

Are they fluffy?
Do any of them resemble an animal? what animal? OR,
    is it a make-believe animal?

Have you ever seen dark gray clouds blackening the sky? What do you think it means?

Have you ever seen clouds that look as if they weren't moving at all and some that were moving very fast?

Have you ever seen rays of sunshine try to peek through the clouds?

241. Did you ever think about your eyes and how wonderful it is to have them?

Just try walking across the room with your eyes closed!

242. Draw these things with your eyes closed:

a ball
a house
your mother
"you"

How did your pictures turn out?

243. If you should spot a butterfly, don't just see how beautiful it is. Stroll about the yard with your eyes on the butterfly to watch it flutter around the flowers.

Do you think it may be sipping some nectar?

244. Have you ever looked down from a bridge? Have you ever seen:

rooftops of houses?	people fishing?
farming areas?	railroad tracks?
boats sailing by?	

cars whizzing by (Has anyone ever honked at you?)

245. Have you ever realized all the different colors fruits are?

yellow (bananas, grapefruit)	green (watermelon, pears)
orange (oranges, apricots)	brown (pineapples, kiwi)

purple (grapes, plums)   red (apples, strawberries)

Can you sort out vegetables into colors too?

246. How many of these things have you ever seen:

A pansy? Does a pansy flower look a little like a face?
Can you see its eyes, a nose, and a mouth?
Raindrops on a window?
A bird enjoying a shower right in the middle of a water
sprinkler?
An insect that looks as if it's all legs? (It's a millipede.
Touch it gently with a blade of grass and watch it
wiggle.)
A black locust tree in bloom? (What a feast for eyes!)
How streetlights (and stars too) seem to twinkle?
Pictures on stamps like: flowers, animals, trees, famous
people? Would you like to start a stamp collection?
Apple seeds, orange seeds, grapefruit seeds. Did you
ever see a pea seed? (It's round so try to roll it
around!)
A round clump attached to some bare branches in the
wintertime when the trees are bare? It's a bird's or a
squirrel's nest!

HEARING

247. What sounds do you hear right now, this very minute?

248. Drop different things, like:

a spool   a penny   a pebble

into a can and hear the sounds they make.

249. Does it ever seem to you that sometimes some sounds go
on forever? Such as:

SENSORY WONDERS

when music that you don't like plays on and on and
on?
when people are clapping for their favorite singer?
after a good speech?
when someone is scolding you for doing something
wrong?

250. If you didn't see, but heard someone in the house
singing or talking—would you know if it was:

your mother or father?   a grandparent?
your sister or brother?   a visiting friend?

251. Have you ever noticed that at every single place and at
every different time of day, there are different sounds to
hear? Such as:

in your house	at the farm	at meetings
in your backyard	at church	at synagogue
in the woods	in the park	at the store

And no two sounds are ever exactly alike!

252. Shh—shh—be very quiet. Do you hear footsteps?

253. When you hear pigeons on a fire escape
or sparrows chirping away
or starlings that sound like busy town gossips

STOP a few minutes to enjoy them.

254. Did you ever hear two squirrels sounding as if they were
having a very important conversation?

255. Are you tired? Then sit on your doorstep and just listen
to the sounds you hear. Do you hear:

church bells?   a radio from an open window?
a fog horn?   lawn mowers whirling?

children skating?
busses rumbling?
a factory whistle?

brakes screeching?
the neighbor's baby crying?
Mother calling you in to eat?

256. Did you ever hear a dog growl and show its teeth? or sniff around another dog?

257. Shh—shh! Is there a rustling in the pile of dead leaves? Is it a lizard? a chipmunk?—or (maybe) a mouse?

258. Can you make these sounds with your voice?

talk	hic-cup	whisper	sniff
sigh	growl	laugh	cough
cry	hum	pant	
giggle	sneeze	snore	Can you gulp?

259. Did you ever hear a balloon burst?

260. How many of these fine "artists" have you heard sing?

the cheep cheeping of the sparrow?
the coo cooing of the pigeon?
the pip pipping of the robin?
the cuckooing of the cuckoo?
the twit twitting of the starling?
the rat-a-tat rat-a-ting of the woodpecker?
the caw cawing of the crow?

Did you ever wonder what the world would be like if there were no birds to sing?

261. What sounds do you hear at a construction site?

drills drilling?
hammers pounding?
bosses shouting instructions?

a worker whistling?
machines sputtering?
saws buzzing?

262. What is the quietest thing you can think of that is happening? Could it be:

a soft gentle breeze?   frost forming on the window?
snow falling?   a cat sleeping on a rug?
grass growing?   leaves falling from a tree?

263. One of the best things about eating an apple is to listen to the crunching between your teeth. (Does applesauce make a crunch? a baked apple?)

264. Do your teeth make sounds? your tongue? your lips?
Can you snap your fingers?

265. There are some very special sounds that tell you some very special things. Some sounds are indoor sounds and some are outdoor sounds. What do these sounds tell you:

the police officer's whistle?   church bells?
an ambulance?   a fire engine siren?
the telephone ringing?   the doorbell?
the kitchen oven timer?

What does the alarm clock tell you in the morning?

266. Isn't it interesting to think about water and all the wonderful sounds it can make? Have you ever heard:

your faucet dripping?
a river flowing gently? or raging?
a rippling brook?
the roaring of a waterfall?

The next time it rains—listen. Is the water gushing out of the water spout or is it trickling out?

267. Usually, our stomachs are pretty quiet considering all the work they have to do; but, all of a sudden—did you ever hear your stomach growl?

268. Would there be anything you would like more than to sit on your parent's lap to hear:

a story about fairies, animals, and giants?
stories about when your parents were young? (especially if they lived in faraway countries)
stories about when you were born?
just a made-up story about anything?

TOUCHING

269. Do you like the softness of:

a cushioned chair?   a pillow?
a gentle breeze?   a baby's cheek?
. . . what about a bedtime kiss?

270. We all know that fingers feel things. But do you know that tongues can feel too? Try feeling these things with your tongue:

an ice cube
toasted bread and untoasted (Can your tongue feel the difference?)
cold water, hot water
dry cereal, cooked cereal

How does frosting on a cookie feel?

271. How would you feel

If you rolled on the grass or a gentle grassy slope?
If you could take a walk in a soft, gentle misty rain?
If you got caught in a rainstorm and got wet through and through?
If it were snowing and you could touch a snowflake that landed on your jacket?
If you were caught in a spider's web?

272. Has gum ever stuck to the bottom of your shoe? How did it feel?

273. No two different animals feel the same to your touch.
Touch your dog.
Touch your cat.
Do you have a pet rabbit?
Do you have a pet garter snake you can touch?
Do you think an elephant feels like a shaggy buffalo?
Did you ever want to touch a peacock's feathers?

274. What would hurt you more:

falling on a rug?   OR
falling on a sidewalk?

275. How do your hands feel when you are out in the freezing cold making snowballs and snow people?

276. Feel your dog's nose.
Does it feel hot? cold? warm?
How does your nose feel?

277. Feel a handful of corn before it is popped. Then feel it after you make popcorn.

278. Where would you rather sit when it's very hot outside?

in the sun?   or   under a shady tree?

279. When you come home from shopping, feel the

potatoes	brussels sprouts
apples	watermelon
cauliflower	cantaloupe

oranges   lettuce

Each one feels so different. Did you ever think about
that?

280. Did you ever touch your adam's apple? Touch it
when you talk
when you blow
when you sing a song
If you can whistle, try that too.

281. When you go barefoot in the house, does every floor feel
the same?

How do the tiles feel in the bathroom?
How does the kitchen floor feel?
Do you have a wooden floor in the living room, or
does it have a soft woolen rug?

282. How does it feel to have an ice cube melt in your hand?

283. Have you ever:

fallen off a tree?   accidentally touched some
been pricked by a pin?   cactus needles?
tripped on a sidewalk?   stubbed your toe?
bumped a wall?

How does it feel? Did it make you say "ouch"? Did it
make you want to be more careful next time?

284. Tickle someone with a piece of dried grass. They didn't
mind it, did they?

285. Close your eyes. Use just one finger.
Can you tell what you are touching? Is it:

a bracelet?
a spool of thread?
a clothespin?
prickly pine needles?

a can of soup?
a marble?
blunt scissors?
your stuffed bear?

286. It feels so good to turn acorns over and over in your hands.

>Acorns are also good for stuffing in pockets or for playing store.

>Did you ever see a squirrel with acorns stuffed into its cheeks?

287. Make a tempting "Feelly Book" or "Feelly Collage" from a collection of:

milkweed pods
dried flowers
pebbles
teasel

shells
pinecones
bird feathers
dried insects

leaves (smooth, scratchy, fuzzy)
bark (Please don't remove the bark from living trees; doing so could hurt them.)

288. Which feels hardest to chew:

white bread
rye bread   OR
whole-grain wheat bread?

289. Do things feel the same when they are wet as when they are dry?

>Does a wet washcloth feel the same as a dry one?

>Does your hair feel the same when it is wet as when it is dry?

>Does a mop?

>Does the earth in your garden?

>Does the laundry?

290. Walk in your father's shoes or your mother's heels.

TASTING

---

291. How many ways have you tasted potatoes?

raw	baked	boiled
hashed brown	french fried	in potato salad

What about potato chips? potato skins? potato soup?

292. Have you ever noticed that food tastes better on an empty stomach than a full one?

293. Can you taste the difference between whole milk and skim milk?

Did you ever taste buttermilk?

Some people are allergic to cow's milk, so they drink goat's milk. You might taste goat's milk sometime to see if you like it.

294. Have you ever played near ocean water?

If you get a spray of it or a bit on your arm, taste it.

Is it salty?

295. Don't look. Taste a spoonful of these seeds. Can you tell which of them you are eating?

hulled pumpkin seeds	sesame seeds
poppy seeds	sunflower seeds

296. Chew some of these snacks if you are "craving" something to eat. They're healthier for you than cookies and cake:

popcorn (plain)
shredded wheat or puffed rice
vegetable slices (carrots, celery, etc.)
fresh fruit (apples, pears, grapes, etc.)
peanuts (You can make your own peanut butter if you
can have someone watch you use a blender.)

297. Have you ever stopped to think of all the different parts of
a plant we eat? (roots, stems, buds, fruit, leaves, the tuber)

Which part do these foods come from?

beets	apples	lettuce
beet greens	potatoes	broccoli

298. Does a cooked carrot taste like a raw carrot?
Does a baked potato taste like a raw potato?
Does canned orange juice taste like fresh orange juice?
Does a plain slice of bread taste like a piece of toast?

299. How fortunate we are that when Europeans came to
America, they brought buckwheat with them. Taste
these dishes and you'll know just how lucky we are:

buckwheat cereal
buckwheat pancakes (yummy!)
buckwheat stuffing for chicken
kashe (roasted buckwheat with an egg and then boiled)
kashe varnishkes (a great combination of kashe and
noodles!)

300. Taste a bit of these herbs and spices on your tongue.
Have you ever used some of them in cookies?

sage	thyme	ginger (It's easy
cinnamon	mint	to tell this one
nutmeg	basil	in gingersnaps.)
cloves		

301. Did you ever go swimming in a pool and accidentally get a taste of the chlorinated water? Ugh!

302. Can you name foods that taste wet, such as an orange?
Can you name foods that taste dry, such as bread without butter?
Can you name foods that taste squishy, such as a banana?

303. Crying brings tears to your eyes. Really cold weather can bring tears to eyes. So can onions. Did you ever taste a salty teardrop?

304. What wonderfully tasty breads there are. Have you ever tasted these breads?
white bread, whole wheat bread, rye bread, cornbread, banana bread, pumpernickel
Did you ever eat Matzo? (This is a Jewish holiday bread.)

305. Can you taste the difference between a salty salad dressing and one that has tangy lemon squeezed into it?

306. Have you ever tasted:
crisp raw pea pods?
clean white snow just fallen from the sky?
olives? Do you like them?
Have you ever had berries on your cereal? Don't they make the cereal delicious!
cream cheese on a hot bagel?
Instead of water, have you ever had:
apple juice   pineapple juice   grapefruit juice
grape juice   prune juice
lemon juice (Did you ever have a lemonade stand?)
Have you eaten dried fruit like raisins, apple rings, and prunes?
Do you like the taste of onions?
Millions of people around the world eat yogurt. Some

people have yogurt instead of ice cream. You might even like it better than ice cream!

307. Put a bit of these sweet foods on your tongue. Are you able to tell one from the other without looking?

sugar   honey   corn syrup
maple syrup   molasses

308. People all over the world have been eating beans for thousands of years. Here are some for you to taste someday:

from China: bean curds and sprouts
from Mexico: chili and fried beans
from Cuba: black beans and rice
from England: pease porridge
and, from the United States: boston baked beans!

309. Next time you eat lettuce, spinach, or cabbage, remember that you are eating leaves!

310. Do you like these ice cream flavors?

vanilla   chocolate   strawberry
toffee   walnut

Why not try a flavor you have never tasted before!

311. How many ways have you tasted corn?

corn-on-the-cob   cornmeal bread
cornmeal muffins   cornflakes
cornmeal pancakes

Have you ever tried delicious tortillas?
How about popcorn? (This is especially good when you're at the movies.)

312. Does all water taste the same?

Does water from your city or town taste like water from another city or town?

Did you ever taste well water on a farm?

Have you ever tried filtered water that comes in a jug?

Many people have filters installed on their kitchen faucets.

Try bubbly seltzer water.

SMELLING

---

313. A jar of crushed rose petals
   lilac petals
or   violet petals

   is one of the most beautiful smells in the world.

314. A field of clover is probably one of the most precious things on earth anyone could possibly smell.

315. If your eyes were closed tight, do you think you would have any trouble knowing if the store you just passed was a chocolate shop?

316. When an apple falls from a tree and you polish it on your sleeve, have you ever felt like saying "Umm, You smell *so* good!"

317. Have you ever smelled smoke from a house fire? burning leaves? a campfire? cigarettes or a pipe?

318. Is there a smell that makes you want to eat right away—so much, you can hardly wait?

319. Did you ever smell lilacs in bloom?

320. Without peeking into backyards, can you tell which neighbors are having picnics?

321. Notice how nice and fresh a baby smells after a bath.

322. Smell your new shoes. Do they smell the same as your old ones?

323. When you come in from the outdoors, can you tell what you will be having for dinner? (fish? freshly baked bread?)

324. Do your parents have an herb garden?
After a soft rain or even just a light breeze—smell the smells of the mint, bay leaves, chives, basil, and parsley.

325. Put together (one or more) of these spices in a jar and enjoy their fragrance:

cloves   cinnamon   nutmeg
allspice   mint

326. When you see clover, bend down and get close to it to enjoy its sweetness.

327. Did you ever smell honeysuckle on the vine?
Does it almost "take your breath away"?

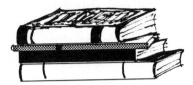

328. Are there some old musty books stored away in the old musty trunk in the basement? Do you like the musty smell?

329. When you're driving to the farm, smell the dust of the country road. Does the hayfield have a smell? the barn? what else?

330. Can you smell the difference between sour milk and fresh milk?

331. Take a little walk down the block. How many different smells do you smell?

any garden flowers?

grass that was just cut? (Can you almost smell the green of the grass?)

pollution? (gas from cars and trucks)

wild honeysuckle coming to you on a breeze?

a twig from a pine tree? (Do you care to bring it home so the family can enjoy its fragrance too?)

the smell of fresh paint on a neighbor's house?

332. Are there any smells that make you:

| happy? | sad? | mad? |
| afraid? | sick? | |

Ask your parents this question and see if they come up with different answers.

333. Ask someone to let you smell different objects while your eyes are closed. Maybe your friend can find such things as perfume, an onion, chocolate, mothballs. See how many you can identify. No peeking!

334. Did you ever think about what a wonderful sense of smell that bees must have—to be able to smell blossoms wherever they are, to get pollen?

335. How many of these smells have you ever smelled?

A clean lake?   a polluted lake?
a field of clover?   coffee, tea?
mothballs?   gasoline?
a letter with perfume on it?
an old pile of dead leaves or an old rotted board?

Did you ever smell buttered popcorn? Yummy!

PHYSICAL WONDERS

MY SHADOW

I have a little shadow
*   that goes in and out with me,*
And what can be the use of him
*   is more than I can see.*
He is very, very like me
*   from the heels up to the head;*
And I see him jump before me,
*   when I jump into my bed.*

The funniest thing about him
*   is the way he likes to grow—*
Not at all like proper children,
*   which is always very slow;*
For he sometimes shoots up taller
*   like an India-rubber ball,*
And he sometimes gets so little
*   that there's none of him at all.*

He hasn't got a notion
*   of how children ought to play,*
And can only make a fool of me
*   in every sort of way.*
He stays so close beside me,
*   he's a coward you can see;*
I'd think shame to stick to nursie
*   as that shadow sticks to me!*

One morning, very early,
*   before the sun was up,*
I rose and found the shining dew
*   on every buttercup;*
But my lazy little shadow,
*   like an arrant sleepy-head,*
Had stayed at home behind me
*   and was fast asleep in bed.*
—Robert Louis Stevenson

336. How many pennies can you toss into a tin can? shoe box? or

a hat that's upside down?

337. Did you ever go "bowling"? All you need to do is stand soda pop cans in a row or turn paper cups upside down and see how many you can knock over by rolling a ball into them.

338. Line up these targets in a row and see how many bottle-caps or stones you can land in them. Use any one or all of them!

a waste paper basket   a cardboard box
a big mixing bowl   paper grocery bag
a pail

339. When you're at the beach, be sure to let the waves tickle your feet and also "skip" a flat stone in the water.

340. You can "nest" anything that can fit into something else. For example, you can nest:

pots and pans   mixing bowls
empty cans   and even shoes and hats!

341. You'll love swinging and swirling from a thick, knotted rope that is hung from a strong tree branch.
(A barrel is good to swing in too!)

342. Did you ever walk barefoot on soft, cool grass?
Did you feel every bump and every tickle?

343. Hang a bell from a tree branch and see if you can toss a beanbag up to it to hear it ring.

344. The big fat log is waiting for you to
walk across it   OR
get up on it to jump down from!

345. Do the refrigerator,
the bathroom floor,
the sidewalk, OR
the porch steps
need a painting? (Of course they do!)
Then get busy! Get out your paintbrush and a can of water!

346. Blow bits of tissue paper and see where they land.

347. One of the very best and least expensive toys anyone in the whole world could have,
whether you are one, two, three, four, five years of age and (yes!) until you are "big,"
is a big bunch of scrap wooden blocks that you can get from a lumberyard OR
a set of wooden blocks made of 2 x 4 lumber sawed into different lengths.
(There is nothing that these wonderful blocks cannot make!)

348. When you go for a walk, see how far you can go without walking on a sidewalk crack!

349. Look about an abandoned construction site, and you may (if you're very, very lucky) find a wooden cable spool. See if you can get it home, because it's wonderful for crawling through. (Ask an adult to help you with this—it's easier and safer that way!)

350. When you climb up the grassy hill in the nearby park—is it almost like climbing the highest mountain in the world?

351. Can you creep like a cat on your tiptoes and fingertips? Can you creep all the way from your room to the kitchen and surprise Mother with a meow-meow?

352. Can you keep a balloon in the air by patting it with your hands?

> Can you keep a balloon in the air by patting it with your hands and not letting it touch the floor at all?
> Can you toss it in the air and hit it with your head?
> Can you blow it from one end of a table to the other side?
> Can you blow a balloon from one room to another?
> Can you play volleyball by patting a balloon over a string from one side to another—again and again?
> Can you get a balloon to float in the air? for how long?

353. It's such fun to sit on the floor with your friend, spread your legs apart, and just roll a ball back and forth to each other.

354. You're all by yourself? There is no other child to play with? Then try playing with:

an old unused typewriter
a magnifying glass
miniature cars, furniture, dinosaurs
some unwanted clothes
an old unwanted adding machine, clock, radio, or cash register

or would you like to "read" a book?

355. Can you twist your body one way and then another?

> Can you twist your body while you walk?

356. Make these items into "mountains" and then knock them down:

pillows	cans
stones	empty milk cartons

See the crash they make! Do they all sound the same?

357. Make yourself tall and straight. Now make yourself small and round.

358. You can start to be an Olympic walker by walking just a little faster (and faster) in your yard and then going down the street.
   Would your friend like to do this with you?

359. When it's windy out and most people are indoors, go out just to walk against the wind.

360. Ask your parents to hang a soft ball (like a beach ball or a foam rubber ball) from a branch of a tree so you can swing it back and forth.

361. Go "camping" with some soft, warm blankets on the floor by the window—and watch the night begin to fall.

362. Just about every child in the world has played tag—but did you ever play tag by walking instead of running?
   Did you ever call "safe" by touching something made out of wood?
   or squatting? or freezing like a statue?
   or touching a fire hydrant?
   Instead of tagging someone with your hand, tag with a buttercup or a pretty stone.

363. You don't always need a party to play "Pin the Tail on the Donkey." You can play it anytime. And you don't need to use a tail or a donkey. You can put:

an apple on a tree
a spider on a web
or a trunk on an elephant

a pocket on a kangaroo
a tusk on a walrus

364. If you have a big beach ball and if you feel a little silly:
Kick the ball backward.
Waddle with the ball between your ankles.
Kneel and push the ball with your forehead.
Can you think of any other silly things?

365. Fly a kite.
(If you don't have a kite, you may enjoy a helium balloon tied to your belt as much or almost as much.)

366. You can play a regular game of dominoes; but dominoes are
also good for making houses, skyscrapers, and stairs too!

367. Have you ever realized that every single walker walks in
a different way? Have you seen some walkers swinging
their arms high and low? and some with their arms very
still at their sides?
Have you seen some walkers walking very fast and
some who just sauntered along?
Have you seen some take big giant steps and some,
tiny mousy ones?
Some just look down, and some keep their heads high!
How do you walk?

368. How many out of ten clothespins can you drop from
your nose and land into an empty can at your feet?

369. If you have a wagon, go for a ride in it.
Give your friend a ride in it.
Can you give two friends a ride in it?
Play "train" with your wagon (and be sure to collect
your "train fare"—some stones—for rides).

370. Instead of a candle for "Jack be nimble,"

> have Jack jump over a book.
> Then another book.
> And another book.
> How many books can Jack jump over before they are knocked down?

371. Did you ever "skate" on paper plates?

372. Have a great time in the snow by making piles of snow-balls and trying to hit a target. Trees make great targets.

373. How far can you walk with a potato on a spoon? Can you walk:

> across the room?
> around a chair?
> under a yardstick laid across two chairs?

374. Did you ever spin a yo-yo?

375. You don't need to buy a special mat for the floor for tumbling when you can just as well use an old mattress or some folded blankets.

> A mattress or blankets are also good for trying out cartwheels and just rolling back and forth to music.

376. You don't have a snow-sled or a toboggan for going down the slope?

> Do you have a piece of heavy cardboard? a garbage can lid? a tray?

377. Of course a wading pool is for wading in, but it is also good for seeing how many acorns you can pitch into empty margarine containers that are floating in it.

378. How many of these can you do:

skip	run	fall	leap
trip	slide	dance	jump
stumble	stamp	hop	waddle

379. How good are you at doing this: Lie on your back and see if you can lift your body on your hands and walk backward!

380. When the oatmeal is all gone, don't throw the box out.
    Just roll it along with your feet
        anywhere you want to go.

381. Can you take apart and put together again a double boiler (including the cover)   OR
a percolator coffee pot?

382. Cut out some square shapes of cardboard, put them in a line, and walk from one to another. Then:

jump from one to another	run from one to another
skip from one to another	hop from one to another

383. What are some things you can do with one cardboard square? Can you skip around the square?
    jump over it?
    touch it with your elbow and your knee?
    kneel on it and pull yourself along?

384. Can you do a somersault?
    Can you somersault across the room?

385. Do you know how to play ticktacktoe?
Do you know that you can play ticktacktoe outdoors on the sidewalk with some chalk?

386. Is there a tire that isn't needed? It would be good for jumping or hopping in and out of.
If there are lots of tires, put them in a line and jump or hop in and out of them.

387. Have you ever played "stone school"? It's a perfect game for playing on steps.
All you need is a stone and someone to be the teacher.
The teacher will hold the stone in her fist and you guess what hand it's in. If you guess the correct hand, you can go up the step.
If you don't, you stay "put" until you guess right.
(Of course, you begin school on the bottom step and keep going up—till you graduate!)

388. How high can you leap?
Can you leap over someone who is in a crouched position?

389. A most superior sand set can come right from your kitchen. Nothing in the world is better than

spoons or measuring spoons	a colander
cups or measuring cups	a funnel
pots and pans	the flour sifter!

390. You can be a kangaroo by holding a ball between your knees and making:

> short little jumps
> longer jumps   AND
> sideways jumps.

391. You can be a tightrope act at a circus if you walk on a long string or put masking tape on the floor.
(Be careful so you don't "fall off" and get hurt!)

392. Can you hop on one foot—then another?
Can you hop high and then hop low?
How far can you hop with your arms folded?
Would you like to have a hopping race with your friend?

393. Be a grasshopper.
Hold one foot in your hand   AND
hop on your other foot.
Can you do it?

394. When you crawl, both your hands and your knees are on the floor.
How far can you crawl? through your whole house?
Can you crawl under someone's legs?

395. When your dog runs, you be a dog too and run along with him.

396. Play "kick ball" by yourself.
Just kick it   AND
go get it.
Then kick it again—and again!

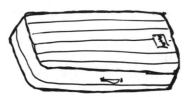

397. Don't throw out an old mattress. Put it down in the basement for:

jumping up and down on   OR
taking a little rest from playing hard.

398. Can you pour dry cereal from one cup to another without spilling any?
Can you pour water from one glass to another without spilling any?

399. How many of these things can you do:

Make your arms go around like a windmill.
Stand and stretch on your tiptoes.
Wriggle your toes.
Squint your eyes.

400. Is it snowing outside? Take a walk down the street or around the block and see the white world.

401. Putting gravel into piles for mountains—
breaking up the mountains—
and making mountains all over again
is one of the greatest pleasures of all early childhood.

402. Walk with your knees high in the air. Can you run with your knees high up too?

403. How many sit-ups, push-ups, or toe touches can you do in one minute?

404. Any home can have a bridge to go under if
you lay a table leaf or a flat wooden board across some
books or boxes.

405. You can have a "scavenger hunt" anywhere—in your
home, your backyard, or when you're at the park. All
you need are things to hide like pinecones, an old shoe,
an apple, and so forth—and a friend or two to find them.

406. How many of these things can you do with a rope:

Can you walk on it as if it were a tightrope?
Can you jump from side to side of it without touching
the rope?
Can you hop from side to side without touching it?
Can you make the first letter of your name with it?

407. How many things can you do with a ball?
Can you put it on top of your head and catch it when it
falls off?
Can you throw it up in the air, clap, and catch it?
Can you bounce a ball, twirl around, and catch it?
Can you roll it?
Can you throw it? underhand, overhand, or with two
hands?
Can you catch a ball? a high ball? a low ball?
Can you bat a ball? dribble one?

408. You don't have a store-bought basketball hoop to play
with?
Then take a bicycle wheel (with the spokes taken off)
and
attach it to a pole.
(It can be just as much fun for tossing balls into!)

409. Can you rub your head and pat your stomach at the same time?

Can you pat your head and rub your stomach at the same time?

410. You can move many ways while you are standing in one place. Can you stretch?

bend?   twist?   sway?   shake?

411. Piles of dirt, stones, and gravel are all you need for

hauling   loading   dumping

They are also good for making pies, cakes, as well as

castles   roads
caves   and a hundred other things

412. Invite the neighborhood children to take part in a big parade that would go around the block with bicycles, wagons, tricycles, or skates. Maybe the parade could be for a cause, such as peace or ending hunger.

413. Is there a low branch on a tree?
Climb up to it.
If it's especially sturdy, hang from it.

414. Make a snowman and dress him up with a man's hat, a pipe, a man's belt, and so on.
Then, make a snowwoman with a woman's hat, a purse, and so forth.
Add some little children.
Then make some snow pies for them to eat!

415. If you don't have a volleyball net, make your own net with a string or rope tied between two poles or two trees.

416. A stick is

to drag—   to poke into holes—
to drop and pick up—   to ride "like a horse"—
    and
to fish for whales with in a "sea"!

417. Stand with your feet apart, stretch your arms forward and upward, and slowly stand on your toes to

reach for the sky
reach for the birds   AND
reach for the tall trees growing

418. Try this with your friend: Lie on your back—feet to feet, push up with your hands or elbows, and say "Hi" to each other.
Then "go back to sleep" and do it again.

419. You can do so many things with a hula hoop. Try these:

Hang a hula hoop from a tree and toss a ball or balloon through it.
Have someone hold up a hula hoop and you run through it. Then have it held higher and higher.
Hold a hula hoop in front of you. Can you jump through it?
If you have more than one hula hoop, lay them on the ground and walk through them, run through them, or hop or jump through them.
Leap through them like a frog that jumps from lily pad to lily pad.

420. If you have a wagon, a bicycle, a tricycle, or anything with wheels—it's a lot of fun to turn them upside down and spin the wheels.

421. Sometimes it's fun to take a walk with Mother or Dad and go nowhere very special—
just the two of you—
just so you can talk together.

422. How tall can you make a tower from pots and pans, sauce pans, and frying pans?

423. Backyards are usually places where you can play safely—but, if you have no backyard, there are some other possibilities:

garages
steps
play yards for apartment
    buildings
school yards

front and back porches
neighborhood parks
driveways that could be
    closed off for safety
a vacant lot

Sometimes the city will close off a street and open fire hydrants for children.

424. If you have a wagon, pull it,
        or
would you like to give your friend a ride in it?

425. All the wonderful things one big carton (from the new stove or refrigerator) can be:

a mountain
a space ship

a fort
a skyscraper

a house
a pirate ship

426. Ask someone to make a trail of chalk arrows on sidewalks, fences, and so forth, and see if you can follow it.

427. How many ways can you get from one side of a room to the other side? Can you:

walk softly like a cat? fly like a bird? crawl like a worm?

428. After you have rinsed off a paper dinner plate, see how many times you can sail it through a suspended wire clothes hanger.

429. A leaf, a walnut shell, or just a mayonnaise jar lid makes a fine boat to sail in the bathtub water.

(If you use a jar lid, be sure the rim side is up!)

430. Put a book on your head and see how far you can walk without its falling off.

431. How good are you at picking up a pencil just with your toes?

432. Anyone can play a toss game anywhere—even if you're sick in bed. You can toss:

cards into a box
buttons or pennies into a muffin tin
rolled-up socks into a waste basket (Be sure to fish
   them out!)

433. Tree stumps are for being "kings" and "queens" of the "mountain."

Is there a stump in your backyard or at the park?

434. Can you carry a teaspoonful of water across the room without spilling it?

435. Does your park have a wading pool?
(Did you ever find any lost pennies in one?)

436. Can you walk on your toes? run? dance and go round and round?

437. Can you skip forward?
Can you skip backward?
(Be sure you look back first so you don't bump into somebody or something!)

438. To play "Follow the Leader," all the players behind the leader must do whatever the leader does. If the leader waves arms, hops, or jumps up—you have to do it too. If you don't, you're out!

439. When you go on a nature scavenger hike, be sure you collect only things that you can return safely and without damage. Here are some possible items to search for:

a feather
a thorn
an eggshell
something sharp
something perfectly straight
something beautiful
a maple leaf
a chewed leaf
something white
a cicada's shell
something fuzzy

440. Did you ever step into someone's footprints in the snow and follow them to see where the person went?

441. Do you know how to make a sockball?

Just roll up a pair of socks (even if they don't match), and tuck them inside the top of one of them

or

hold them together with a rubberband.

(If you want a bigger ball, use more socks.)

Sockballs are good for playing with indoors or outdoors.

You can toss a sockball back and forth with a friend.

Try it overhanded.

Try it underhanded.

Move farther away from each other and see how far you can throw it without dropping it.

Try passing a sockball along from one person to another and see how long this can be kept up without dropping the sockball.

442. For a first-class obstacle course, you need some or all of these:

a barrel to crawl through

a rope to shin up

a tree limb for throwing a ball over and catching it on the other side

a narrow plank set on two bricks or a board over two boxes

a pile of leaves or newspapers to jump over

443. If your parents don't have a spoiled tire, ask your nearby gas station attendant for one.

A tire is glorious for a tree swing for the backyard,

or

if the tire can be sliced in half, the one half would make a fine "box" for sand, dirt, or gravel, and the other half could be filled with water for "playing boat."

444. A bottom kitchen drawer is a ready-made storage area for some of the best playthings any child can have:

pots and pans (and covers)
measuring cups and spoons
wooden spoons
sieves
mixing bowls
food scrapers

445. If you have the money, it's easy enough to buy toys at a toy store, but can you buy the most wonderful toys of all in "nature's gift shop"? Such as:

stones	pinecones
walnuts	sticks
feathers	sea shells
pebbles	acorns

These gift stores are all around—in your backyard, at the beach, at the park, on your way to the store.
You can:

fill muffin tins with the pebbles
pour walnuts in a shoe box and take them out again
put acorns in a small hole cut in a shoe box top
make a train from stones
and so many, many other things!

446. If you stuff pillowcases with crumpled newspaper you can have an "inside snowman." Then make some crumpled newspaper balls to see if you can knock his head off. (It's O.K. to knock off the head of a snowman.)

447. How many ways can you move? Can you:

flop	kneel	roll	slide
lie down	stretch	tiptoe	skip
leap	turn	hop	sit

dance round and round?

448. Just about any hike one can go on is fun. And there are so many different ones too, like:

A breakfast hike:
> Hike to where you can see the sun rise and eat your breakfast.

A star hike:
> Hike to look up at the stars and wonder.

A nature hike:
> Hike to see all the beautiful things of nature about. Maybe you can pick a flower or find a pretty leaf to take home.

A rain hike:
> Put on your rubbers and raincoat and see what happens to plants in the rain and if any animals are about.

A stream hike:
> Follow a stream as far as you can.

An overnight hike:
> Hike for a long time and find a perfect spot to set up your tent to sleep in overnight.
> Or just use a blanket to spread out for your sleeping bag.

An Indian hike:
> Hike quietly and one behind the other, looking.

A sniffing hike:
> Hike to smell flowers, bark, and underneath stones.

A color hike:
> Find flowers that are yellow, blue, or any other color. Enjoy the different shades of green of the leaves.

A seed hike:

Collect seeds and bring one or two home to plant.

A bark hike:

Find bits of bark that have come off the trees. See how many different kinds of bark there are.

A cooking-out hike:

Bring food along with you and eat along the way.

A zig zag hike:

Make sudden turns to side streets, turning corners, going down streets you never went down before.

A curiosity hike:

Go when your parents have lots of free time. Go nowhere special—to the park, down the street, into the neighborhood, not going in a hurry, not pressing forward, being curious, looking, smelling, touching the world!

IMAGINATION WONDERS

What can you do
What can you do
What can you do
With a bed
Paint it red
Paint it red, yellow and blue
And paint the covers too!
Paint purple, orange and brown on it
And then jump up and down on it!
Oh, no! No! No!
What are beds really for?
That's right!
Good night . . . sleep tight!

Please don't correct me . . .
Let me draw the way I feel . . .
Let me pretend . . .
I know you want to help me
But just as soon as you want me to do it your way—
I begin to feel it's no use trying and
I begin to feel bad about myself.

449. Can you roll up like a ball and tumble like a tumble-weed?

450. If you had a red bandanna—would you want to be a cowboy (or a cowgirl)?
   Would you care to lasso a pony?

451. Can you waddle like a duck?
   Can you crawl like a snake?
   Can you hop like a frog?
   Can you leap like a kangaroo?

Can you swim like a fish?
Can you gallop like a horse?
Can you swing like a monkey?
Can you creep like an ant?
Can you soar in the sky like a bird?
Can you walk like you?

452. What are three things you can do with:

a rope?   a nut?   an old hat?
a feather?   a stick?   a handkerchief?
a paper bag?

453. Walking is almost like talking with your feet.

Walk as if you were enjoying a warm summer afternoon.
Walk as if you were in very deep snow.
Walk as if you were in a terrible hurry.
Walk as if you were tired.
Walk as if you were dizzy.
Walk as if you were very sad.
Walk as if your shoes were too tight and hurt you.
Walk as if you were walking in an icy cold stream.
Walk as if the wind were blowing hard.
Walk in mud that feels gooey, sticky, and squishy.
Walk very quietly as if the baby were sleeping.

Can you strut and gobble like a turkey?
How does a baby walk?

454. Pretend to be a snowball melting away in the sun and ending up as a pool of water.
Pretend you're a kitten waking up from a long nap.

455. Be popcorn popping in a pan.
Pretend you're a tree bud opening up.

456. How do you say "Where are you going?" as if you were:

> your mother and she was very angry
> talking to your little puppy
> a police officer or security guard

457. Be an elephant and sway your trunk.

> Be a slithering snake.   Be a bear lumbering along.
> Be a squiggly worm.   Be a spider spinning a web.
> Be an eagle soaring   Be a buzzing bee.
>   through the sky.

458. Have you seen seeds blowing through the air in the springtime? Can you act out this old, old rhyme?

> "Thistle-seed, thistle-seed
> Fly away, fly!
> The hair on your body
> Will take you up high.
> Let the wind whirl you
> Around and around.
> You'll not hurt yourself
> When you fall to the ground."
> —*Author Unknown*

459. Be the wind and blow softly . . . more . . . more . . . more . . . less.

460. What are three things you can do with a marshmallow (besides eat it)?

461. Suppose you lost your million-dollar necklace. How would you look for it?

462. Make believe you are:

> crossing a stream on a round log or slippery stones

riding a bronco
walking in jungle underbrush
peeling a banana and eating it
walking on ice
throwing and catching a ball
driving a truck
threading a needle
taking off your shoes and going to bed

463. Supposing you were the world's greatest pianist (or violinist) performing at the finest concert hall in the world.
How would you come out on stage?
Let's see how you play the instrument.
What do you do before you leave the stage?

464. Can you be a bride by using an old curtain?
a famous dancer by using one newspaper with fringes cut out at the bottom?
a fairy princess by using a bit of tinsel?
a lion tamer by using a piece of rope?

465. There are lots of things you can do with a stick or branch you found on the ground.
Can you drag it?
Can you poke it into old newspapers and make holes?
Can you ride it like a horse?

466. Be a butterfly: Spread out your wings—and look for nectar.

467. What are three things you can do to make your mother smile?

468. "Talk" without words. Say:

I'm happy.
I'm sad.

I'm tired.

I'm lost in the store.

My zipper doesn't work.

It feels so good when Mother puts a bandage on my sore finger.

469. Can you dance like a dragon?
Can you sing like a dragon?
Can you laugh like one?

470. How many things can you make from just one stick of modeling clay?

471. Can you show without speaking that:

your stomach hurts?   your toe hurts?

What other part of you can hurt?

472. Can you be a ballet dancer? Be sure to twirl and kick your legs high in the air. Whirl and whirl over again—Wheeeeeeeee!

473. Can someone guess what you are pretending to open? It is helpful if you do something with the object. For example, if you open a box of candy, take out a piece and eat it. Then show how you like it! Try these:

Open a safety pin.
Open a letter.
Open a package of groceries.
Open the garage door.
Open an umbrella.
Open a package of chewing gum.

Open a box of crackers.
Open a can of paint.
Open a cantaloupe.
Open the zipper on your jacket.
Open a jar of peanut butter.

474. Count to ten as if you were:

angry   happy   sad
very smart   shy   silly

475. Would you like to be someone other than YOU for a little while?
Be a "firefighter" with a raincoat.
Be a "nurse" or a "doctor" with a piece of hose for a stethoscope.
Be a "teacher" with a story book.
Be a "house painter" with a brush.
Be a "hairdresser" with scissors (but not sharp ones).

476. What would it be like to be a snowflake?
Can you float through the air like a snowflake?
Can you hit the ground?
Would you like to be packed into a snowball or made into a snowperson?
Would you want to melt into water?

477. Can you be a witch combing her long stringy hair?

478. Pretend you are walking barefoot:

on hot pavement
through a big water puddle
through prickles
in deep snow
through tall grass

How would you walk barefoot in chocolate pudding?

479. Can your finger wave "good-bye"?
Can your finger tickle you?
Can you scratch your hair with your finger?

480. Can you pretend to be:

someone fishing?
someone sewing?
someone sawing wood?
someone hoeing the garden?
someone feeding chickens?
someone hanging the wash?
someone polishing shoes?
someone pushing a wheelbarrow?
someone picking flowers?
someone sweeping the walk?
someone getting dinner ready?
someone driving an automobile?
someone rocking the baby to sleep?

481. Can you pretend you are:

a pitcher warming up to throw a ball?
Father shaving?
an older sister brushing her hair?
your little brother throwing a temper tantrum?

482. Pretend you are quiet things like:

a statue   a rabbit   a whisper

483. Accidents can happen to anyone. Make believe you:

stubbed your toe
bumped into a wall and banged your nose
stumbled over a rock

Suppose you accidentally fell into a hole?

484. Pretend you are a tire pumped up.
Pretend you are a table tennis ball in the middle of a
    game.

Pretend you are a monkey swinging from a tree.
Pretend you are a typewriter.
Pretend you are an old, old man walking.
Pretend you are a bowl of jello.
Pretend you are a flower—growing.
Pretend you are crossing a busy street.
Can you pretend you are a yo-yo?

485. Walk like a giant.
Walk like an elf.
Walk like YOU.

486. Can you act like a mean person who doesn't like children?
Can you act like a person who loves children?

487. Someday—would you like to be a big brown bear and sleep in a cave until the snow begins to melt?
or
Would you like to be a baby bear—getting washed, eating, and then going outside to play?
or
Would you just care to waltz with a bear,
tumble with one,
go hopping with one,
or go sailing with one?

488. Be the captain of a boat by using a nutshell and a pan of water.

489. Pretend you are:

a ball   a doll   a robot
a windmill   a rocking chair

490. Make believe your finger is a teacher and she or he is giving a lesson on how to use the word "please."
(You would rather listen to a finger than to someone giving you a big lecture—wouldn't you?)
Can the "teacher" give a lesson on:

"standing straight and tall"?
"how to brush your teeth"?
"how to be a good sport"?
"not talking to strangers"?

491. Pretend you knocked over an expensive vase!

492. How do you look when you feel

flippy?   whoopy?
fizzy?   whizzy?

493. Can you be a swimming camel?
a flying dog?
a whale in a goldfish bowl?
a walking pencil?

494. Can you imagine the taste of a banana?
the sound of crunching an apple?
the smell of clover?
what a crocus looks like when it peeks out of the snow?
the feel of your mother's cheek?

495. Be a turtle and dig in the sand in the sun.
Be a fox and run in the tall grass.
Be a robin and sing to your babies in the nest.
Be a chipmunk and play by a sycamore tree.
Be a honeybee humming in her hive.
Be a mother beaver and build a dam of sticks.

Be a frog and swim in a green, wet bog.
Be a spider and spin a web in a pine tree.
Be an owl and wink because it's getting late in the day.

496. If you roll a piece of tissue into a ball and put this inside the middle of another piece of tissue—you can have a *ghost!*

497. Wouldn't it be fun to make a paper-bag mask for everyone in your family?

498. How do you act:

when you don't get enough sleep?
when you eat too much?
when you have a toothache?
when you can't go outside because you've been naughty?

499. All the wonderful things and people you can be:

Be an engine as in Watty Piper's *The Little Engine That Could.*
Be Madeline as in Ludwig Bemelmans' *Madeline.*
Be Mike Mulligan as in Virginia Lee Burton's *Mike Mulligan and His Steam Shovel.*
Be a cat in Wanda Gag's *Millions of Cats.*
Pretend you are a little ant or a little train too, just as in Lois Lenski's "The Little Ant and the Little Train."

500. Can you pretend to be an elephant sneezing?

501. Can you be a tree all curled up in a seed?
Then grow a little at a time to be a grown-up tree.

Sway your leaves in a gentle breeze.
How do your leaves move in a terrible windstorm?
What if someone cut you down!

502. Pretend you are your mother or father.

503. Be an explorer and walk down a dead-end street.

504. Can you make your body do all these things?

Make yourself round.
Make yourself as tall as possible.
Move only one part of your body.
Make your body as quiet as possible.
Reach as far as possible.
Be as short as you can. Be as tall as you can.
Tremble like a leaf.
Slink like a cat.
Crawl like a snake.
Wiggle like a worm.
Be a rabbit, a bear, a grasshopper, a spider.

505. Pretend you are a bird. What would you do if it rained?

506. Say "Today is Monday" (or whatever day it is) as if you were:

happy	scared
sad	bored
mad	lazy

507. Next time you see a fuzzy caterpillar, ask him if he knows he will be a butterfly someday.
When you see a tadpole, ask him if he knows he'll someday be a frog.

When you see a baby, does she know she'll grow up to be a big person?

508. Do you know that hands can talk? How do they say:

"Come here."
"Stop."
"Enough."
"Just a little."

How do they lead an orchestra?

Do your eyes "talk" too?
What can they say?

509. How do you act when you are scolded for a messy room?
How do you act when you get a compliment for your nice clean room?
How do you act when it's rainy and you can't have a picnic?
How do you act when it's nice and sunny and you *can* have your picnic?

510. Can you be things that move? Such as:

a train	a roller coaster
a wheelbarrow	a bus
the moon	

511. Does your parent have an old unwanted Sears catalog? Pretend you are ordering your wardrobe for school, for a party, or for a trip you are going to take.
Select furniture for your "dream house."

512. How do you think you would feel if you woke up one morning and found a zebra playing on your front lawn?
if an airplane landed in your backyard?
if you found a turtle in your bathtub?

513. You don't know how to read yet? Then just look at pictures and make up your own story.

514. Can you act out this little rhyme:

"Hippety-hop to the candy shop
to buy some delicious candy.
One for you, and one for me
and one for sister Mandy."
—*Anonymous*

515. Some Mother Goose rhymes are especially good for pretending. Rhymes like:

Little Bo-Peep   Jack and Jill
Humpty-Dumpty   Little Jack Horner
Simple Simon   Little Boy Blue
Lucy Locket   Little Miss Muffett

516. Can you swim like a fish and then nibble a worm on a hook?
fly like a bee, buzz, and sting someone?
peck and scratch at food like a chicken?
soar in the sky like an eagle?

517. Can you be a roaring lion, pacing back and forth?
Can you be a polar bear, rolling over a few times and then falling asleep?
Can you strut like a peacock and let everyone know how beautiful you are?

518. Make believe you are doing these things and see if someone can guess what you are doing:

tagging   chinning
catching   galloping
dribbling   sliding
batting   kicking
skipping   throwing
                            and doing a cartwheel

519. Can you act out sadness? Such as:

when a picnic is canceled because of rain
when someone dies
when you see Mother cry
when you lose your allowance
when you fall off the bicycle and get hurt

520. Did you ever feel like lying in a bed a little longer? Then pretend your bed is a boat and you can be the captain.
What can the pillows be? the blanket?
What will you do if a sudden storm appears?

521. If you had a long piece of material, could you:

wind it around your head for a turban?
wear it as a cape and be Superman?
tie it around your waist and be a baker with an apron?
put it around your shoulders and be an old woman
    with a shawl?

522. A string or rope around some pieces of furniture can be:

> your dungeon
> cage
> jungle
> or castle

523. Make believe you are yawning and do this until someone else yawns!

524. Can you pretend you are a bee visiting flowers? or a puppy playing with a cat? or a giant walking through the earth, shaking the earth and knocking down trees?
Would you like to take a ride in a big balloon?

525. Be Jack-Be-Nimble and jump over the candlestick. See if you can hop, dance, walk, or skate over the candlestick too!

526. Can you act out these words?

sleeping	jumping
exercising	bowing
rocking	bouncing
shaking	balancing
climbing	reaching
drooping	swimming
shivering	stumbling
knocking	leaping
hopping	falling
whirling	dancing

Can someone guess what you're doing?

527. Can you be a weeping willow tree?

528. If you wore a large brown paper bag or a box with holes cut out for the face and arms—who would you want to be?

a knight?   an astronaut?   a dragon?

or would you just feel like wearing it and being nothing in particular?

529. Pretend you are a radio or television reporter and talk about the weather, the traffic, or what's "on" for the day. Or, you can be a disc jockey and play some of your favorite songs.

530. Can you dance like a dragon?
Can you sing like a dragon?
Can you weep like a dragon? laugh like one?
Can you roll over on the ground like a dragon?
(You can do all—or almost all—of these things if you try!)

531. Without using words, have others guess what you are doing:

petting a cat   making snowballs
talking on the telephone   getting dressed
tasting some baked cookies   typing a letter
feeding the birds   sweeping the floor
reading a book   playing the flute
rocking a baby in my arms

532. Make believe you are smelling a flower, picking it, and giving it to a friend to smell too.
Make believe you are walking your dog.
Make believe your shoes are stuck in the mud.
Make believe you are putting on roller skates and skating for your very first time.

533. Can you pantomime these directions?

March in step.   Clap your hands.
March in high step.   Turn right.
Kick up right foot.   Turn left.
Kick up left foot.   About face.
Swing your arms.   Open the door.
Jump up and down.   Tiptoe.
Do somersaults.

534. Make believe you are light things like:

air   dandelion seeds
marshmallows   dust
facial tissue

535. Make believe you are heavy things like:

a jug of milk   mud
iron   rocks

536. Stuff an old unwanted pillowcase with newspaper to be your new friend to keep you company. Would you like your friend to be a cuddly dog?

537. Pretend you're:

an ice cube   a hot potato
a baby rabbit   a salamander
a sticky sweet roll

538. Pretend you are something or someone who moves slowly. Such as:

a turtle walking
an alligator sunbathing
an old, old person

539. Make believe you are eating:

> an ice-cream cone that is melting
> a caramel apple
> very hot soup
> a sour pickle
> a spoonful of "yucky" medicine!

540. Can you picture what it would be like if:

> every flower in the world were pink?
> spinach tasted like ice cream?
> dogs sang? and birds barked?

541. Show me how your

> eyes say, "I'm surprised!"
> chest says, "I'm proud."
> finger says, "Come here."
> nose says, "I've got a cold."
> ears say, "Listen to the birds."
> hands say, "Stop!" "Go!"
> head says, "No," "Yes."

542. You don't know how to read yet? Then just look at pictures and make up your own story.

543. What happens to:

> a hat   a windmill   a kite
> clouds   a sailboat

> when the wind blows?
> What happens when the wind goes to sleep?

544. Bark like a dog.
> Meow like a cat.
> Hop like a rabbit.

Roar like a lion.
Can someone guess what you are?

545. Can you dance a happy dance? a sad dance? an angry dance? a wild dance?
Dance like a rabbit, a skunk, or a cat.
Dance like spooks on Halloween night.

546. Can you be a frog jumping from lily pad to lily pad?
Can you swing like a pendulum in a grandfather clock?
Can you pretend to carry three chairs balanced on your nose?

547. Can you run in slow motion (like the replay of a videotape)?
Can you walk like a crab in slow motion?
How does an elephant run in slow motion?
What about a robot? How does a robot run in slow motion?
What if a clock ticked in slow motion?
Could you eat an ice cream cone in slow motion?
Could you *really?*

548. Pretend you are a bright, twinkling star shining on the earth. Show how stars make you feel—
so still
so beautiful
so quiet
so very, very quiet.

549. You can be anyone in the whole world if you want to be. Would you like to be someone in these stories?

Would you like to be a little pig in "The Three Little Pigs"?

Would you like to be Goldilocks in the story of Goldilocks and the Three Bears?

Would you like to be Red Riding Hood? or the Little Red Hen?

Would you like to be the witch in "Hansel and Gretel"?

How would you like to be the Gingerbread Boy? Rapunzel?

An elf in "The Shoemaker and the Elves"?

Rumpelstiltskin?

Sinbad the Sailor?

Paul Bunyan, who weighed more than fifty pounds when he was born and was about five hundred feet tall?

How would you like to be Rip Van Winkle and sleep twenty years?

Would you like to be the Sorcerer's Apprentice?

550. Would you like to be someone other than YOU for a little while?

Using a raincoat, be a "Firefighter."

Using a piece of hose for a stethoscope, be a "Nurse" or a "Doctor."

Using a storybook, be a "Teacher."

Using a brush, be a "House Painter."

Using a comb, be a "Hairdresser."

Using a pan, be a "Cook."

Using a badge made from a round piece of foil, be a "Police Officer." Using a straw hat, be a "Farmer."

Using a letter, be a "Postal Worker."

Using high heels, be a "Fashion Model."

Using some old shoes, be a "Shoe Cobbler."

Using a can and cartons, be a "Store-Keeper."

Using a stick for a wand, be a "Fairy Princess."

Using an earring, be a "Gypsy."

551. Pretend you are a cow chewing her cud.

Pretend you are a cat catching a mouse.

Sit down like an old, old woman.
Walk like a marine.
Cry like a little baby.

552. If you need to live in a cave

or

a lion's den,
throw an old sheet or blanket over the kitchen table.

553. Can you "talk" without words and say:

I'm happy?   I'm afraid?
I'm sad?   I love you?
I'm tired?

554. Can you imagine the sound of:

a zipper?   a twig breaking?
a fire burning?   a baby laughing?
popcorn popping?

555. Pretend you're puzzled about something and scratch your head to show it.

Pretend you're happy about something and clap your hands.

Are you hungry? Rub your tummy.

Are you frightened?

556. What could you be if you had:

a long coat?   a necktie?
your dad's or mother's shoes? costume jewelry?
a scarf?   old kitchen curtains?
an old tablecloth?   a whistle?
a bath towel?   an old broom?
an old pair of glasses?   a big twig?

557. Just about everyone knows these stories. Would you like to pick one for you and your friends to act out?

"Chicken Little"	"Sleeping Beauty"
"The Little Red Hen"	"David and Goliath"
"The Boy Who Cried Wolf"	"Rip Van Winkle"
"The Three Little Pigs"	"The Leak in the Dike"
"Little Red Riding Hood"	"William Tell"
"Three Billy Goats Gruff"	"The Gingerbread Boy"
"The King of the Golden River"	"Cinderella"
"The Hare and the Tortoise"	"The Fir Tree"
"The Ant and the Grasshopper"	"Rumpelstiltskin"
"The Ugly Duckling"	"Goldilocks and the
"The Pied Piper of Hamelin"	Three Bears"

558. Here are some "Pretend Kits" for times your friends come to visit you.

Hospital Kit: Includes small plastic bottles, pieces of tubing for stethoscopes, cotton balls, raisins for medicine, etc.

School Kit: Includes pencils, paper, chalk, rulers, books, blackboards, etc.

Play House or Restaurant Kit: Includes pots and pans, measuring spoons, boxes for tables and chairs.

Grocery Store Kit: Includes cans, boxes, pretend money, etc.

What Am I? Kit: Includes dark glasses, wigs, false teeth, make-up, etc.

Cleaning Kit: Includes rags for dusting, brooms, mops, sponges.

Post Office Kit: Includes used letters, used stamps, stamp pads, etc.

Beauty Parlor Kit: Includes hair rollers, mirror, combs, hairbrushes, etc.

Ice-Cream Parlor Kit: Includes empty ice-cream cartons, plastic spoons, napkins, etc.

Baby Kit: Includes plastic bottles, rattles, dolls, etc.

559. Here are some things you can "play" in your backyard with your friends:

Play "Pet Show" and everyone can bring their pet or pets for the great event. (Dead butterflies would be fine too!)

Play "Library" and collect books, comics, records, and magazines to lend out. Maybe you can arrange to have a story hour too.

Play "Fashion Show" using a collection of old dresses, scarves, hats, jewelry, long skirts, pocketbooks, and high heels. Be sure to play the right kind of music for the modeling.

Play "Circus." You will need a ringmaster, clowns, an acrobat—and a tightrope walker. (This tightrope will be on the ground, of course!)

Play "Bakery" with a collection of old cookie sheets, muffin tins, measuring spoons—and a white bag for the baker's hat.

Play "Show" with plays you or the other children make up. Be sure you practice how to make bows and curtain calls that come after the applause.

Play "Restaurant" with some small tables and chairs—or boxes will do too. Serve juice and health cookies or crackers. You will need a main chef and waiters or waitresses.

Play "Art Gallery" with great works of art created by you or others in the neighborhood. If you sell any (a penny or two would be a good price) you could buy some seeds and give them to someone who would like to have a garden.

Play "Post Office" and sell stamps, weigh packages, and so forth.

You can play "Junior Olympics" and play jacks, jump rope, or have some races.

Have a "World's Fair" and show a collection of your foreign dolls, show pictures of things made in foreign countries—also show pictures of foreign people and places. Do you have any foreign records you play?

Play "Store" with empty cereal boxes, milk cartons, shoe boxes, cans, and so forth. If your mother has any kinds of leftovers, you can use those too. You can be a storekeeper, or would you prefer to be a customer?

Have a "Talent Show" where anyone can show off anything special he or she can do. You can be a great musician—even a rubberband that's plucked is a fine instrument to show off. Can someone play a guitar?

HELPING WONDERS

LATER

Mom always says,
"Clean your room."
I say, "Later."
She always says,
"Wash the dishes."
I say "Later."
My sister says,
"Get off the phone,
It's my turn."
I say, "Later."
Sometimes I put off life
For later
And just dream.
Mom says,
"Turn off the TV."
I say, "Later."
Mom says,
"I love you.
Come give me a kiss."
I say, "OK."

—Aliya Hart

560. A fun job to have for every day is to fill the water dish for the cat or dog and watch them dash for it.

(Would you like to help the birds outdoors with a water dish for them too?)

561. Clotheslines are usually too high for little children to hang the wash on,

but

can you help by handing out the clothespins as they are needed?

562. If you pick some peas or beans from the garden—
   you'll be very happy when Dad announces at the table,
   "Steve picked them all by himself!"

563. When you have the job of watering the houseplants
every day—
   you also have the extra good feeling of watching them
   live and grow!

564. Do you know what to do when you see that the wastebasket is all filled up?

565. Is the sick tree being cut down? (How sad.)
   Can you help pick up the fallen branches,
      rake up the chips and fallen leaves,
         and
         sweep up the sawdust?
   (Then, can you help plant a new tree?)

566. When the newspaper carrier brings the newspaper to
your outside door every day—
   would you like the job of bringing it inside every day?

567. In the early spring, can you help plant the seeds in the
vegetable garden?
   (In a little time they will sprout, and soon the whole
   family will have good things to eat!)

568. Help brush door and window screens and hose them
down so they will be all ready to hang in the springtime.
(How appreciated it will be when the flies and the mos-
quitoes start coming around!)

569. Not only is it fun to help shape the hamburgers, but you
will enjoy them a lot more at the dinner table if you do!

570. Do you know what to do with your bathing suit and towel after swimming or any kind of water play?

571. Be helpful and save all the buttons you can find and put them in the button box. (Someday someone may need one just like the one you found!)

572. Listen to those beans snap when you get them ready for dinner!

573. You know why a knife should be handed to another person with the handle first—don't you?

574. Do you take your dog out for a run every day?
If your neighbor isn't well
or is very, very old
or has a disability
or is very busy,
    can you take his or her dog out for a run too?
(Don't forget that the dogs must be on a leash and also
    don't forget the scooper for the droppings!)

575. How much litter can you pick up with
a long sharp stick
        or
a stick with a nail at the end of it?
Did you ever try picking up litter with giant-sized tongs?

576. Do you help keep mud and dirt out of the house by scraping your feet on the outdoor mat before coming in?
(Do you know that in some countries—nobody—*nobody* can come into a home without taking shoes off? Some go barefoot and some put on house slippers, which

wait at the door! How would you like this idea at your home?)

577. Do you have the same job to do every day
over
and over
and over again?
Would you like to switch jobs with your sister or brother for a day?
a week?
for "good"? Would your parents allow you to do this?
Would your parents allow the children to pick slips of paper from a hat that list "jobs to do"?

578. There are lots of other uses for an egg-timer besides timing eggs for boiling.
Can you brush your teeth till the sand runs down?
Can you get dressed all by yourself before the sand runs down?

579. Here are some ways to help your neighbor:

Can you pay her a visit sometime and find out if you can run an errand for her?
Can you take her paper to the door?
After a heavy snowstorm, can you shovel a path for her?
Can you bring over some flowers from your garden or share your crop of grapes with her?
When she's resting in the afternoon, can you do only quiet things?

580. Cleaning your room can be a lot easier and a lot more fun if you have bushel baskets—

one basket for blocks and other toys
one for "dressing up" clothes

and a third one for things that need to be washed

(Each basket could be a different color so you can tell one from another. They also make your room look prettier!)

581. If Mother is in the kitchen
and
Father is in the basement—
can you bring a message from one to the other?

(For example: If Mother wants you to tell Dad that dinner is ready and to come up to eat—can you do it?)

582. Help prepare dinner by scrubbing potatoes and carrots (and other vegetables that grow under the ground) with a scrub brush. This will make them nice and clean so you can eat the skins that are so delicious and so healthful too!

583. How many ways can you help make the birthday cake?
Can you help measure the flour?
Can you help sift the flour? (Do you have a hand sifter?)
Can you measure the sugar and add it to the batter?
What about the raisins,
the nuts,
and the *frosting?*

584. After a snowfall, get out your shovel and help shovel the snow.
(Snow shoveling by little children does not have to be done in a systematic way!)

585. Dirty hands carry a lot of unhealthful germs.
Do you have the habit yet of washing your hands
before you eat
and

before you handle food?
(It's one of the best habits anyone can have!)

586. How many of these jobs can you help out with for the camping trip? Can you:

help prepare the foods to bring?
help gather the pots and pans and some camping supplies?
shake out the tent and sleeping bags?

When you get to your campsite—at night—
can you help build the campfire for roasting marshmallows?

587. Picking up debris about the front of the house (and back of it) is more fun when you put the debris in your little red wagon
and then
dump it into the trash can.

588. How would you like the very important job of sweeping the kitchen floor
and
putting the sweepings into a dust pan every day after dinner?
(Everybody would really appreciate it!)

589. When a toy is used, the grown-up thing to do is to put it back in the toy box when you're done.
When you're finished looking at your book, do you put it back on the bookshelf?

590. Would you be able to cube or crumble the bread stuffing for the turkey all by yourself?

How proud you will be when it's announced at the dinner table, "Eric helped to make the stuffing!"

591. Can you put on and take off a buttoned shirt?
a buttoned sweater?
a buttoned coat?
If they have zippers instead of buttons, can you zip them up and zip them down?
What about snaps? Can you work snaps? Can you tie your shoes?

592. All of us love parties—but parties can be even more fun if we help out with them.

Can you help prepare the refreshments?
Can you help make the decorations and party favors?
Can you help prepare the entertainment by thinking of a pretty song to sing?

593. It seems that lots of people don't like to clean the garage or the shed.

Wouldn't it be nice if you offered to help clean it?
(You might find a nickel there or the ball you were looking for!)

594. There are always so many jobs to do about the house. How your parents will love it when you say "Give me a job to do now!"

Would you like to help sort out the paper clips, pins, and safety pins?
Would you like to feed the guppies?

Would you like to help load and unload the washing
machine and the dryer?
Would you like to roll up the socks?

595. Wouldn't it be fun to help make a window flower box
a trellis for the roses
or
a tree house for the backyard?

596. See if you can get permission to pick some garden flowers
or
find some pretty wildflowers to put in little vases
about the house. (They would help make the house
so cheerful!)

597. Do you lay out your clothes for the next day before you
go to bed?

598. Can you help get the salad ready for dinner by twirling the
spinach and lettuce leaves with the hand salad-spinner
or
would you rather help dry the leaves with a dish towel
or paper toweling?

599. Do you know how to use the fire extinguisher?

600. Do you know how to use the pencil sharpener?
Can you collect all the dull pencils,
sharpen them,
and put them back—all ready to use again?

601. Would you like to help fill your home with smiles?

Plan a surprise for Mother's going back to school.

Fix up and decorate a spot with a mural.

Invite the new child down the block to meet your family.

Share a little poem you made up with the rest of the family.

Why not do an extra chore without being asked?

602. When you go camping:

Do you help pick up the litter and put it in the trash can, so you can leave the site as clean as the way you found it?

Do you keep your radio and voices down—especially at night when others might be trying to sleep?

(Besides, loud noises drown out the quiet sounds of birds and little animals.)

603. Do you have an old hand potato masher you can use to mash the potatoes to make them soft and fluffy to eat?

604. A hammock strung between two trees in the backyard is for any child who helped clean the garage on a hot summer's day.

Do you think it "pays" to be helpful?

605. People buy centerpieces for the table, but everybody would enjoy it much more with a centerpiece you made all by yourself. Like:

a daisy in a jar
some dried flowers
a leaf in a cup
or
a picture you drew

606. Are you able to dust-mop the whole living room floor by yourself,

shake the dust out of the mop when you're done,
and
hang it up where it belongs so it will be ready for "the next time"?

607. Do you think you should walk around your neighbor's lawn or walk across it?
Of course, you would want to walk around it so as not to wear a path through the grass.
What are some other ways to show you care about preserving your neighborhood?

608. Can you help your parents plant the new shrub in the garden
or
the new hedge along the driveway?

609. If your sister isn't feeling well,
do you think she would enjoy being served breakfast in bed?

610. It's good that peanuts have soft shells and are easy for children to crack (and to munch on too).
But for pecans, almonds, and walnuts—
can you use a nutcracker?

611. You know the tune to "Here We Go Round the Mulberry Bush"—don't you?
When you are helping to clean the house—can you make up words about what you are doing that go with that tune?

612. Would you be able to
prepare a pan of warm water and soap suds,

and wash, rinse, and put out your dolls and doll clothes to dry?

613. Can you help spade the vegetable and flower garden? (If you get tired doing it—play a little while, then go back and spade some more.)

614. Empty pots and pans in which eggs or cereal have been cooked are much easier to clean if—
they are soaked in cold water first
THEN
washed with soap and water,
dried,
and put away.

615. When the groceries are brought home, can you help bring them into the house and put them where they belong? Doesn't it make you feel grown up to help?

616. Bathroom floors and bathroom walls are often made from shiny tiles that are so easy to keep clean.
When you see a dirty spot, can you wipe it off with a bit of water on a cloth?

617. You are very helpful when you can go to the library and return borrowed books.
You can be still more helpful at the library. For example: When you speak, speak quietly so you don't disturb others who are reading.

618. When everyone is finished eating would you be able to:

get up from the table, carry one dish at a time to the sink,
and scrape it—WITHOUT BEING TOLD?

619. Are you a zoo keeper?
　　Do you feed your pets
　　　and
　　clean their cages every day too?

620. When your dad is working in the backyard and needs the rake or some other tool—can you get it for him?

621. If some of your friends pitched in to help you clean the backyard—would you give them each an apple to show your appreciation?

622. Cutting and pasting things always seems to make such a mess.
　　Can you pick up the scraps and put them in the wastebasket?
　　(If you can learn to do this when you're very young, you'll do it when you're grown up too!)

623. Can you pour water from a pitcher into a glass without spilling a single drop?
　　Can you do this for everyone at the dinner table every night?

624. When you find toys strewn around all over the backyard,
　　do you pick them up and put them where they belong?
　　(Can you do this without being told?)

625. The best thing about helping out is that it can bring two persons closer together.

626. It's very helpful to have a good reminder like a "Daily Check-off List" for your daily jobs. It could include:

Did I make my bed?
Did I clean up my room?
Did I brush my teeth?
Did I lay out my clothes?

Would you also like to have a "Weekly Check-off List" for weekly jobs like helping to water the garden, cleaning out the car, changing bed linens, and so forth?

627. What are some ways that you can help birds?
Where winters are cold and birds have a hard time finding food, can you help to make them a bird feeder?
(Once winter birds find food they will keep coming back to your feeder. So be sure to put food in the feeder regularly until spring. When spring comes, they will be able to find their own food.)
Birds like to bathe if water is nearby. (It's not always easy for birds to find a place to bathe.) Can you help make a bird bath?
In the spring, can you help put out things birds need to build their nests? Like:

string
cotton pieces
brightly colored yarn

628. Can you make your own orange juice from that old hand orange juice squeezer and some real oranges?
(You'll find it tastes a lot sweeter and better because it's really fresh and pure
and
you made it yourself!)
Can you make some for your parents this way too before they go to work?

629. You're lucky if you have your own room to sleep and play in.

   Do you put all your toys away when you're finished playing with them?

630. On a hot summer's day, it can be a lot of fun to help Mom or Dad wash the car with a bucket of soapy water and a sponge.

631. When you help clean the garage, basement, or the attic— you may be surprised at the collection of things you'll find that the family doesn't need anymore. Things like:

   clothes that are too small
   toys and games that no one uses anymore
   unwanted furniture
   old records

   Can you pass anything on to a friend or neighbor?
   Can you use anything for a garage sale?
   Can you donate some things for the homeless?

632. Your parents will praise you for being "big" if you can "read" them stories while they are doing things such as ironing, shaving, and so on.

633. Have you noticed that when you cook and clean up *while* you are cooking, there is little to clean up later?

   Do you put the mixing spoon in a dish so the table doesn't get too messy?
   Do you wipe up spills right away?
   Do you put dishes to soak as soon as you finish using them?
   When everything is clean and in order, do you sweep the floor?

(Parents will be happy about this and let you work again in the kitchen!)

634. Are the lawn and garden dry? Do they need watering?
Can you help get out the hose and water them?
What about the window flower box? Do you have a watering can?
When you're all done watering, can you help put the hose and watering can away?

635. Are there any bare spots on your lawn?
Will your parents let you help rake it up a bit,
sprinkle grass seeds on it,
and
help water it till the grass comes up?

636. If your little sister or brother is sick in bed—get a pillow-case,
help stuff it with towels or other soft things,
and dress it up with a face and a belt or a hat (if you want one).
Now your sister or brother has a good playmate for lonely times!

637. If the television or radio sets are on and no one is using them, do you know how to turn them off? See how many lights are on in your house. Can you turn off the ones that don't really need to be on?

638. What are some ways you can help:

a senior citizen on a bus?
a mother with her little baby?
a person with lots of packages?
a person who has a physical or mental disability?

639. Do you leave the sandbox and the sandbox area clean and neat before you leave to go indoors?

    If you do, then it will be ready for you next time and you'll be so glad!

640. Are there any spills on the countertop? the table? the floor?

    Can you wipe them up as soon as possible so the spills won't become too hard to clean later?

    (Do you think a spill could cause someone to slip and fall?)

641. After a long winter,

    when the lawn furniture is (finally!) brought out,

    can you help wash it so it can be nice and fresh for the summer's use?

    (If the furniture needs painting, can you help with the painting too?)

642. See how grateful your neighbor will be when you bring over a plateful of cookies that just came out of the oven!

643. Do you know what a weed is? Can you pull out five weeds (one for each finger) in the vegetable garden?

644. Can you put away the knives, forks, and spoons where they belong?

645. Self-starters do what they have to do without being reminded by parents.

    Are you a self-starter?

646. Do you know that one of the best gifts you can give to your parents is the offer to do anything they want you to do?

647. How many of these "helpers" do you know how to use?
Do you know where they are when you need them?

the kitchen broom	the lawn mower
the push broom	the rake
the dust pan	the shovel
the floor mop	the grass clipper
the scrub brush	the spade
the carpet sweeper	washcloths
the vacuum cleaner	rags
the water pail	a sponge

648. If your parents are sending a letter to Grandma
or
sending out a big mailing for a club meeting—could
you help them by:

folding the letter sheets?
putting them in envelopes?
sealing the envelopes?
putting the stamps where they belong?
putting the letters in the mailbox?

649. A dishpan half-full of warm soapy water,
a dishpan half-full of warm rinsing water,
a dishcloth or a sponge,
and just a little "elbow grease"
are all you need for washing the dishes. (Even if you
just help your mother or father do some of this, it
shows that you want to feel "grown up.")

650. Do you know how to make ice cubes
and
remove them from the trays?
(Can you drop an ice cube in a glass of lemonade?)

651. Polishing the brassware, silverware, and copper pots is a
big job for a parent,

BUT
it can go a lot faster and be fun to do
IF
you work together on it.
(Besides, think about all the things you can talk about
while you work!)

652. Do you put your two shoes together and in their right
spot when you take them off?
(You wouldn't want to be like someone who gets mad
when he or she "can't find the other shoe" just
before having to go somewhere—would you?)

653. You can have a "Kids Vacation Service" for neighbors
who go away on vacation by helping to:

water their plants
feed their pets
and
bring in their mail and newspapers

654. When your parents are in the kitchen getting dinner
ready—
could you "help" with a nearby box of old pots and
pans, measuring spoons, and plastic dishes
and
make a dinner for your doll family too!

655. You can help prepare the flour for the birthday cake and
make it fluffy and free of lumps and bumps by using the
hand flour sifter.
(A manual flour sifter is safer for children than electric
ones—and lots more fun to watch too!)

656. Can you pour some cold cereal in a bowl (without
spilling any) and

add the milk (without spilling any)
all by yourself?

657. Can you help Mom or Dad set the table

over
and over
and over again—
till you can set it yourself?

What do you think everyone will think then?
Do you think they will be proud of you?

658. Is it hot and sticky outdoors? Do you think the people passing by and the nearby construction workers would like some lemonade?

Could your parents help you set up a lemonade stand on your front lawn?
Do you think your customers would like some crackers or some cookies too?
(Wouldn't it be fun to be the waitress or the waiter?)

659. Holiday time is usually a busy time, especially if there are fruitcakes and other such goodies to make.

Can you help make the work easier by cutting up the dried fruit—apricots, apples, pears, and peaches?
(You'll be glad you did when you smell the cake baking—Yummy!)

660. Are you going for a trip in the car?

Would you like to help by being in charge of the litter bag for the empty containers, dirty napkins, and scraps?
(When the bag is filled, would you make sure it's emptied along the way and replaced with a clean one?)

661. When something is torn or broken—such as a window, the picture book, or a leg of the chair—or when a light bulb burns out,

do you report it to your parents?

662. Do you know how to sort laundry?

663. Dog houses get dirty the same as people's houses do.

Can you sweep out your dog's house? shake out the bed? and put it in the sun to air out—all by yourself?

664. It would be very helpful if you decorated your family's bulletin board from time to time. You could change it with:

a drawing of your trip
a fern or flower you found
a Van Gogh postcard you bought at the art gallery
or
a mounted sea shell.

665. Answering the telephone seems easy, but it's a very important thing to do correctly.

Are you allowed to answer the telephone?

How would your parents like you to answer?

What do you do when a tape recorder answers the other line?

What do you say when someone wants to speak with your sister who isn't home? Do you know how to take messages?

How would you reach the police station or the fire department if you needed help?

(It might be a good idea to practice answering the telephone on a toy telephone first!)

SAVE-OUR-EARTH WONDERS

666. When you go shopping with your parents, look at containers of the items they buy to see if you can reuse them to store your toys, your stone collection, nails, or other items.

667. They may not seem to be much at the time, but (after a while) drips can add up to lots of water.

Will you let your parents know just as soon as you see a faucet begin to drip?

668. After the laundry is washed, hang it outdoors to dry (even if you have a clothes dryer). Doing so saves energy—and besides—the clothes will smell cleaner and fresher.

669. Do you like to go camping with your parents? Do you pitch in to help clean up your campsite when it's time to go home? (You wouldn't want the next campers to think that litterbugs had been there before them—would you?)

670. If your family doesn't drink soda—do your neighbors? Collect all the aluminum cans you can find for recycling.

671. It may be hard for little children to understand, but all glass jars (mayonnaise, jelly, pickle relish, etc.) can be melted down and made into more jars. So collect all you can. Then, take them to a local recycling center.

672. Of course, a cookie can taste just as good from a paper box as from a plastic one. But wouldn't you enjoy it more if you knew the cookie came from a paper box that could be recycled into more paper boxes?

673. You should treasure those lasagna and spaghetti boxes that have windows on them. They are made-to-order temporary houses for spying on grasshoppers and other insects. Be sure to remove the window before you finally recycle the box.

674. Recycle brown paper bags as:

trash or garbage bags
piñatas
masks (put in eyes and a mouth)
puppets (if you stuff one and fasten on a stick to hold it with)

If you fill a bag with air, would you want to make a big blast by popping it?

675. Dump coffee grounds in the garden. (When composted, they help prevent the soil from getting too hard.)

676. Aluminum foil can be used over and over again if it's washed. How many times can you use the same piece?

677. So you accidentally spilled some water on the kitchen floor . . . then wipe it up with a sponge or a cloth rag instead of paper towels.

678. When you walk along ocean beaches, pick up litter that you see. If litter such as plastic bags were to wash back out to sea, dolphins and whales might eat it and choke to death.

679. When containers for recycling are put in easy-to-get-to and easy-to-reach places, it makes you want to help more, doesn't it?

680. Help gather old newspapers, bottles, cans—anything that can be recycled (especially from senior citizens and neighbors)—and take them to your garage until your parents can go to a recycling center.

How many times can you use the same plastic or paper bag over
　　　　and over
　　　　　　and over again?

Do you like the smell of pollution that comes from a passing car? (Ugh!)

ARTS AND CRAFTS WONDERS

"It feels so good to do things with my hands
And I love to get them dirty.
It feels good because what I make is all mine.
It feels so good—
I don't want to ever stop."

Do you ever feel this way too?

681. Draw a picture of everyone in your family.
Can you do it without looking at them?

682. Suspend leaves from a coat hanger for a leaf mobile. See
how pretty they look floating gently about in a breeze.
(Would you like to have the letters of your name floating about too?)

683. You don't have sheets of construction paper for drawing
pictures? Then draw on:

old newspapers
brown paper bags cut in half
cardboard liners from packaged shirts
corrugated cardboard
paper towels

You can color the daily comics—they are just like little
coloring books!

684. Mud is very good for patting,

pinching,
pulling,
pounding,

and for making pancakes, meatballs, and peas for dinner.

685. The materials of nature that you find "along the way" can often make more satisfying art projects than store-bought materials. For example, here are some ideas to try out:

Attach pipe cleaners to pinecones to make a turkey.
Sycamore seedballs sprinkled with glitter can be hung from a string for holiday time.
If you find some burrs, they can be made into a porcupine.
If you ever want a "bug," use the furry part of the pussy willow shrub.

686. Do you know that every single person in the whole world has a different fingerprint?
Did you ever see yours? Would you like to make a print of yours?
Just press your finger onto an inked stamp pad.
Then press your finger onto a piece of paper—
and there it is!

687. Listen to a record on your record player or radio and just draw the way you feel.
Does it make you want to make long flowing lines?

Is the music so cheerful that you want to use bright colors?

If the music moves fast, does it make you want to draw a train or a car?

What about jiggly music?

688. Dry a single blade of grass in an old telephone book and then see how pretty it looks when you put it on a birthday card you make yourself.

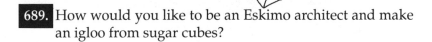

689. How would you like to be an Eskimo architect and make an igloo from sugar cubes?

690. The drawing or the name you inscribe on a growing pumpkin will be so much fun to watch as the pumpkin grows
and grows
and grows
until it is picked!

691. A toothpaste box is just the right box from which to make an alligator.

A tissue paper box can be a boat.

What can you make from a milk carton?

Boxes on top of one another can be a totem pole.

Boxes tied together make a train.

A great big box can be a store or an apartment house.

A lot of boxes of different sizes will make a city.

(Be very thoughtful before you throw out boxes!)

692. A "Junk Box Collection" is a very precious collection of odds and ends for a "what can I do now" rainy, blustery day. It could include things like:

buttons	straws
keys	string
shells	tin cans, aluminum foil
rice	noodles
clothespins	cardboard tubes, boxes, and pieces
tree bark	newspapers
twigs	corrugated paper
safety pins	spools
sponges	masking tape
wood scraps	nuts
photographs	beans
rickrack	tissue paper
toothpicks	scraps of carpet
glitter	old window shades
crumpled paper	greeting cards
scraps of cloth	dried peas
feathers	playing cards
egg cartons	heavy twine
plastic balls	cotton, cotton balls, and cotton swabs
dried flowers	combs
nuts and bolts	old envelopes
bottle caps	old birthday cards
dry cereal	old magazines
seed pods	acorns
pipe cleaners	fur
milk cartons	match boxes
sandpaper	pieces of ribbon
ice-cream sticks	plastic jars and lids
paper bags	old socks of different colors and sizes
old eyeglasses	old pocketbooks
pots and pans	crayons and felt-tip markers
chalk	

Is there anything in the whole world you could not make from these magnificent supplies?

693. Draw a bumpy picture on the bumpy side of corrugated cardboard.

Can you make a log cabin from the corrugated cardboard—or just make some logs?

694. Is there a tree that you like a lot? Then draw a picture of it in the different seasons. Be sure to show:

buds
the color of the leaves and what happens to them from season to season
the leaves falling in autumn
how pretty it is when it's flowering
the apples, if it's an apple tree
a bird's nest in its branches, if it has one

695. Try drawing with wet chalk on dry paper. How does it differ from drawing with dry chalk on wet paper?

Find out for yourself!

696. Here are some colors you can make all by yourself:

For green, squeeze spinach.
For red, berries and beets.
For gold, a marigold.
For brown, coffee grounds.

Does this help you understand how the Native Americans (the Indians) dyed their cloth?

697. Do you have an old unwanted pair of gloves? You can make finger puppets with them.

You can cut off the fingertips and put faces on them with paint or felt-tip markers—and just use the tips
or
you can use the whole glove and paint faces on the tips.

Another way to make puppets is to stick a bandage on your fingertip and draw a face on it. (If you do the same thing on your other hand, you can have the puppets talk to each other.)

698. Make a self-portrait using a mirror.

Now close your eyes. Can you draw a picture of yourself without looking? Can you put in your eyes, mouth, ears, and nose? If you're wearing a hat, you have to put that in too.

(Now—open your eyes AND SEE IF YOU CAN KEEP FROM LAUGHING!)

699. See what lovely "free" pictures you can draw with feathers that are dipped in ink.

700. Draw a picture of the same little brook in the fall, winter, spring, and summer.

701. One of the best things about twigs is that none of them is perfectly straight. Make a "twig collage" of:

bent ones   twisted ones   gnarled ones
and some very funny-shaped ones

702. Do you need a pair of bookends?

Stuff two empty cans with earth
   AND
(if you want to make them extra special)
put in a little plant
   OR
plant a seed in them and watch it grow.

703. Anybody would be happy to save empty spools of thread for you.

Would you like to lace some of them together with an old shoelace to make a wriggly snake? a pull-toy train? a spool necklace?

Spools are also made-to-order for totem poles.

(Did you know that a totem pole—according to Native American lore—is always to be decorated with a special quality of the person who owns it? For example, if the special quality of the person is that he or she is very strong—the design could be that of a lion. Or, if the person is very curious, the design might be a monkey!)

704. A simple and useful gift you can make is a bookmark.

One way is to cut off the lower corner of an envelope (it can be slipped onto the tip of the page to be marked) and make it beautiful by pasting on a tiny pressed flower.

OR

Make a bookmark from a piece of paper or cardboard decorated with a drawing you make.

705. Staple sheets of paper together to make your own notebook for your own trip. As you travel, draw pictures or write about things you see. Your book might include:

a special tree	the windmill
a hill or mountain	a big forest
some baby animal	

The book could be called "_____'s Travel Book."

706. Did you ever try painting with pine needles as a brush?

707. It's very easy to make a paper chain. Just cut out some paper strips all the same size, loop them through one another, and paste together the ends.

Can you make one that will go from one end of the room to another? around the whole room?

Make a chain for any holiday time.

708. Some people have vivid dreams and some do not. If you've had a dream, can you remember it and draw a picture of it?

709. Don't throw out the paper bag. You can make a very fashionable hat by folding it up a little from the bottom and adding decorations (such as a feather or a picture you've drawn of it). Can you write your name on your hat (or have someone help you write it)?

710. Can you paint a bushel basket with a color you like? It becomes a fine storage box for toys. Orange crates also are good to use.

711. Don't get rid of all your cans (like coffee, baby food, and canned fruit and vegetable cans), because these cans are made-to-order for storing:

pencils	paint brushes
crayons	pennies
	and lots of other things!

Of course you could use the cans "as is" after they are washed. But if you want to make them prettier, cover them with colored paper and draw pictures on them,
or
cover them with string or rope glued around them,
or
glue pebbles or seeds onto them.

(You'll see—everyone will want to have one of your storage cans!)

712. Draw a cat or a dog while it's dozing. Shh-shh!

713. If you make sure that the cut-out rims of three, four, five, or more tin cans that fit into one another are smooth and safe, they can be used as a set of nesting cans.

> Boxes that fit into one another can be a set of nesting boxes.
>
> Plastic jars, measuring spoons and cups, and pots and pans can be nesting sets too.

714. Do your parents have any travel brochures they don't need anymore? Then clip the pictures and make a "Far-away Land" book or a collage for your bedroom wall.

715. Draw a map of your house and include rooms where you eat, where you and others in the family sleep, the lavatory, and so forth.

> Can you fill in the rooms with cut-out pictures (or make drawings) of the furniture in the rooms?
>
> Can you make a map of the outside of your house too?
>
> What about a map of the street where you live?

716. Sponge painting is good for

> smearing,
> wiping,
> pouncing,
> trailing,
> > or
> dotting the paint on different textures.

717. The book you make doesn't have to look like a regular reading book. Why not make a Zig Zag book? They're very simple to make—

> You take a long wide strip of paper
> > and fold it in half.
> Fold it in half again.
> > And again and again (if you have a long story).

Then "draw" pictures for your story in each of the sections.

Now it's all ready for you to "read" to a parent at bedtime.

How proud a parent will be of your book! and you too!

718. "Write" a letter to Grandma by drawing pictures and enclosing the letter in a real envelope with a real stamp. (Your parents can address it for you.)

719. For a door that won't stay open, use a brick and paint it or cover it with pretty wallpaper   or

wash the brick well and use it "as is." The color of bricks and their texture are pretty the way they are.

720. Wouldn't it be fun to be a meteorologist?

You can make your own weather chart from a paper plate.

Divide the plate up into different drawings of weather (like rain, sunshine, snow, and so on).

Attach a movable pointer in the center of the plate with a brad.

Then move the pointer to the weather that fits the day.

(Of course, if the weather changes through the day, you will have to keep moving your pointer.)

721. One of the most valuable gifts for any grandparent is an outline of you that someone can make when you are lying down on a big sheet of paper.

(Be sure the details of your face, your clothes, shoes, and other important things are included.)

722. How many different kinds of lines can you draw? a straight line? a crooked one? a wavy line? a zig zag line?

What can you draw from the straight line? a straight tree? a person standing straight?

What can you draw from the other lines?

723. Your parents will surely get more pleasure from the drawings you make for each of the twelve months of the year—than from printed pictures already on a calendar.

Will you have a valentine for February?

a Thanksgiving table for November?
rain for April?
something special for someone's birthday month?

724. A flat stone (about the size of a potato) makes a very good paperweight.
You can wash it and use it "as is"

or

paint all over it with one color

or

attach stripes or polka dots to make a funny mixed-up design on it

or

paint a "happy" or a "sad" face on it.

725. While blindfolded, draw a picture of a flower or a cat.

726. Can you do any of these things with a collection of buttons:

Sort them into different colors? different sizes? different shapes?
"Write" your name with buttons?
Arrange the buttons on a card so they make a pretty picture and then glue them down?
What else?

727. A wind chime, made from shells suspended from a can or coat hanger and hung on the front porch, will give each person who passes by a little treat.

728. Any worn or shabby window shade that still works will look better if it is decorated with a lovely picture you draw. (The picture may also cover up the little holes and the worn parts of the shade!)

729. Can you turn a shoe box into a doll house, a hospital, or anything else you want? Use:

crayons   colored paper
felt-tip pens   rickrack
scissors   paste or glue

730. If you stretch a string or cord across your bedroom wall or use the clothesline outdoors (when it's not used for the wash)—
    you can have your own personal art gallery or a "public" gallery where others can admire your artwork.

731. When you see a silhouette of a beautiful tree against the sky, you must draw it!

732. Corn kernels can make very elegant necklaces. If you let the corn kernels soak a day or two, it will be
    easier to stick a blunt needle and thread through for stringing.
    (Using Indian corn would make the necklace especially glamorous!)
    If you would like to have an appleseed necklace (who wouldn't!), have an adult pour boiling water over

the appleseeds till they get soft and then string them onto thread with a dull needle.

733. You can make a leaf or bark rubbing by putting a piece of paper over the leaf or tree bark and gently rubbing back and forth over it with the sides of a soft pencil or crayon.

You can make "money" rubbings of all coins the same way too.

734. Using different colors of construction paper, cut out lots of big and little circles, squares, rectangles, and triangles.

Can you paste them on another piece of paper to make:

a flower garden?	a house?
a tent village?	a snowman?
a whole city, including skyscrapers?	a tree?

735. Wrap a rubber band around two crayons (or pencils) and draw with them at the same time. Try three crayons sometime!

736. If you find a stone, a shell, or a bone that has a hole in it—you have a special treasure!

Save it,

string a string or shoelace through it, and you have a very special necklace to wear.

737. Would you like to have a scarecrow as a friend who will always be waiting for you when you need her (or him)? Here's all you have to do:

Stuff your old play clothes with crumpled paper, use a balloon for a head (you could put on a face if you wish),

and then plop him or her on a chair to wait for you.

738. If you have any cotton balls or wads of cloth, paint pictures with them instead of using a brush.

739. An old shirt with the sleeves cut off
    or
an old pillowcase with holes slit in it for your head and
    arms
can make a fine artist's smock to keep you clean when
    you do things with your hands.

740. Make a "We All Work Together" book or mural with
drawings you make of:

the mail carrier	the work your mother does
the sanitation worker	the work your father does
the truck driver	your doctor and dentist
and YOU!	

741. Is there a tree in front of the house? Have everyone you
know (your parents, sisters and brothers,
    neighbors, and friends) draw it and see how everyone
    "sees" it differently.

742. If you aren't allowed to go outdoors at night—
    paint a lot of white dots
        or
glue stars on black construction paper
and you will have a sky full of stars.

743. If you need a jewelry box for your rings or pin collection,
you can make one by painting a cardboard egg carton.
An egg carton is also good for storing stones and special
    pebbles.

744. You can make a beautiful holiday wreath from a cardboard circle with a collection of different nuts or pinecones or both, glued around it. Include:

walnuts	hickory nuts
acorns	any other nuts you find

745. If you buy an art postcard every time you and your parents visit the art gallery, you can have your own "art gallery" in your bedroom or on the kitchen bulletin board.

Art posters are usually much more expensive, but maybe you could save your money for these.

746. Can you make a sculpture of "you" from soft mud?

747. Fold a square piece of paper in half.
Then fold it in half again.
Cut out some designs from it.
Open up the folds.
Now you have a pretty snowflake!

748. Everyone will enjoy a "family tree" with photographs beginning with your grandparents, their children, and including you.

If you don't have photographs of some of them, draw pictures of them instead.

749. Make a "moving" mural with pictures you make or cut-out pictures from magazines and newspapers.

Will you include ships, roller skates, motorcycles, wagons, helicopters, and rockets
along with other things such as cars, trucks, and planes?
Will you also include people walking?

750. Do the windows of your house ever get frosty in the wintertime?

See if you can get permission to "draw" pictures on them with your fingers.

751. You're going shopping with Mother or Dad and you don't know how to write or read a shopping list?

But you *can* draw—can't you?

So make a *picture* list of the apples, bread, milk, and anything else that you need to buy.

752. The backs of an unwanted sample wallpaper book can make a deluxe drawing pad for any child's masterpieces. See if you can get one at a nearby "paint and paper" store.

You can also take pages from a wallpaper book and cut them up into pieces that are all the same size. Mix them all up and then sort them into look-alike piles.

753. Have someone use chalk to trace your shadow on the sidewalk when it's sunny outside.

Get into different positions, such as putting your hands on your hips or reaching to the sky—then see what it looks like. What else can be traced?

754. Using your finger and a cookie sheet sprinkled with a layer of flour or cornmeal, you can make a Navajo "sand painting." (Erasing is very easy, for all you need to do is give the cookie sheet a gentle shaking.)

755. When you're at the beach, you'll find shells, pebbles, seaweed, different colors of sand.

Bring some home to make a collage of them

or

glue them onto cardboard for a pretty wall hanging.

756. Can you draw a picture of your face to show what you look like when you're:

happy?	surprised?
sad?	angry?

wondering "what it's all about"?

757. Everyone will enjoy a handprint mural of everyone in the family. Include the baby's handprint too.

Be sure to put names on, so the handprints don't get mixed up.

Also include dates, which are especially important for those who are still growing.

758. Drop a few small blobs of watercolor paint onto a sheet of paper, fold it in half, and press down on it.

Unfold it. You'll be surprised at the lovely twin design you get. Does it look like a butterfly?

759. When you connect paper clips to one another to fit around your wrist, you have a bracelet.

When you add odds and ends like colored buttons or an old key and other such things—it becomes a special "charm bracelet."

760. There is no need to buy puzzles when you can make your own. All you do is find a picture you like in

a magazine and cut it into two, three, four, or more pieces.

Then see if you can put the pieces together the way they once were.

(If you want the puzzle to last a long time, paste the picture on cardboard first—and then cut it out.)

761. Do you see a windmill on your drive in the country? Stop and draw a picture of it so you can show it to your friends. One doesn't see a windmill too often.

762. Make a small sachet (a little bag filled with sweet smells) by stapling two pieces of cloth together on three sides.
Fill it with sweet herbs or flower petals
    and then
staple the fourth side shut.
(A sachet makes the dresser drawer smell so fresh and
    fragrant!)

763. Do you have a photograph of someone you love? Then cut a heart out of a piece of construction paper and place the picture behind the construction paper. Tape the picture in place.

764. Put lots of dots on a piece of paper and connect the dots, going from one to another. Make:

a snake   a person
a flower or a tree   anything

765. Can you draw a picture of "you" with your left hand if you're right-handed? Or the reverse if you're left-handed? Draw a tree or a flower too.

766. How many things can you do with paper? You can:

roll it   fold it   tear it up   pleat it

twist it   cut it up   punch it   crumple it

Can you draw a pretty picture on it?

767. See if you can turn a sheet of newspaper into a wiggly snake by just tearing it. The paper must be torn into just one strip and must *not* have any breaks in it. Tear the paper as thin and wiggly as you like—and then enjoy the snake!

768. You can make some very pretty designs on paper with a paper punch.
   See if you can make a face or a flower.

769. Do you know that no one in the whole world has finger-prints exactly like yours? Would you like to know what your fingerprint looks like?
   Just take your thumb, press it into the ink of a rubber stamp pad, then press it onto a sheet of white paper.
   (If you want to see your print from close-up, look at it with a magnifying glass.)

770. Tubes from:

toilet tissue   aluminum foil
wax paper   or mailing tubes

   can be cut to any size, stood up in a row, and made into cities.

771. To make a log cabin, use a milk carton and cut out a door and windows.
   For the logs, glue on bits of twigs.

772. Have you ever seen "accordion-style" paper dolls? They're so easy to make and you can make a whole pile of them at once. All you need to do is to fold paper accordion-style, cut one doll (making sure not to cut off all the folded edges)—and open it up to see all of them standing in a row waiting for you!

773. Be a designer and draw the outside of your home—and, on another piece of paper—draw the inside of your home.

Be sure to include such things as the:

living room	garage
bathroom	backyard porch
bedrooms	Do you have a garden?

774. Next time you go to a beach and find a hard stretch of firm clear sand when the tide is out—draw a
picture of the waves with your finger or a stick.

775. The easiest turkey to ever make is a hand-turkey. You trace your hand on paper. Your thumb can be the turkey's head, and the fingers, the turkey feathers. Then all you need are a couple of lines for the turkey's feet.

776. Can you make yourself into a robot using a cardboard box with holes cut out for your head and arms?

777. Can you make a "holly-leaf man" from five green holly leaves?

778. Can you make "button people" from a collection of buttons?

779. Make a collage or book of Beautiful Differences, showing people who are:

short, tall, and "middle-ish"
fat, thin, and "middle-ish"
black, white, red, yellow, and "middle-ish"
old, young, and "middle-ish"
factory workers, nurses, mothers, doctors, sanitation
workers, teachers, and without jobs

Show people who can't walk, or talk, or hear, or see, or
think the way you do.

780. Try this:

Fold a long piece of paper about three inches wide
accordion-style.
Draw a picture of a person (be sure the hands touch
both edges of the paper).
Cut out the picture (be sure you don't cut the fold at
the hands!).
When you open the fan—SEE ALL THE DIFFERENT
PEOPLE!
Can you color them with the colors of people? Such as:

black   yellow
brown   red
white

(Isn't it like a bouquet of beautiful flowers?)

781. To make a collage of the colors of people—
trace both your hands lots of times on a huge piece of
paper
and
fill each set of hands with different colors:

black   yellow   white
brown   red

(Isn't it pretty to see?)

MUSIC AND RHYTHM WONDERS

Movement and music is the universal language of children.
It expresses through action
what they think—
how they feel—
and
what they understand.

Wherever you go in this whole wide world,
there will always be little children
who love music and find ways to make music.
Even a child blowing into a blade of grass or blowing across the mouth of a
bottle will find music as lovely as a birdsong.
You be a music discoverer too.
But there is one thing you must always remember—
and remember well and forever:

THERE IS NO RIGHT WAY AND THERE IS NO WRONG WAY
FOR LITTLE CHILDREN TO MAKE MUSIC.
IT'S ONLY JUST FOR YOU TO ENJOY THE WORLD.

782. Can you hum a tune and see if your friend can guess what you're humming?

783. Have you ever stretched an elastic band and twanged some music on it?
Try it.
The sounds will make you laugh!

784. Can you flick a finger against your cheek and play "Row, Row, Row Your Boat"?
Can you snap your fingers to play it?

785. We all know that people talk. A drum can talk too. Listen:

> Hit it with a stick.
> Hit it with your fingers.
> Hit it with your knuckles.
> You can even hit it with your fingernails and it will say something different.

786. What a beautiful hummingbird.
> Move closer to it.
> Reach for it.
> Now the hummingbird is flying away.
> I wonder where it went . . .
> Can you dance with this hummingbird?

787. How would a mouse dance?
> Is he fast or slow?
> Isn't he sneaky?
> See him scamper.
> Is a cat coming?

> How would a lion dance?
> Does he purr like a cat?

> Does he snarl? (It can really scare you!)

> See
> how he stalks.

> Watch how he
> POUNCES.

> Isn't he
> fast?

788. Make raindrop sounds with chopsticks
> or
> crumple tissue paper to make the sound of a million raindrops.

789. Can you dance hiccups?

790. Pick up as much macaroni as you can hold and let it run through your fingers into the macaroni box. What does it make you think of? Rain?
    Swish your hands around in the box.
    Listen to the sounds you make.
    Does that make you think of rain too?

791. How elephants sway and lumber along—
    so slowly—
    plodding—
    swaying like bears—only lots heavier and with trunks.
    Can you dance an elephant?

792. Sing "Yankee Doodle."
    And now sing "Yankee Doodle" holding your nose!

793. All the things birds can do:

    They can fly, hop, swoop, peck.
    See how they soar.
    Some strut.
    Can you dance a bird?

794. Dance and jump to:

    Popcorn goes pop.
    Popcorn goes pop, pop.
    Popcorn goes pop, pop, pop.
    Popcorn goes pop, pop, pop, pop.
    Popcorn goes pop, pop, pop, pop, pop, pop, pop . . .

795. Can you have your drum go fast for a train or a race car?
    Can you drum lightly for

air?   dust?
feathers?   or a dandelion seed?

796. Can you make a dance for each season—spring, summer, winter, and fall?

797. Have a "Whisper Time" at the dinner table—when you can only whisper.
(Even the door has to be closed in the quietest way!)

798. Which of these sounds are usually loud sounds?
Which are usually soft?

a train whistle	shouting	banging	ringing
a sneeze	whistling	squeaking	grating
hissing	booming	whining	tickling
crashing	snoring	buzzing	

Can you make the sounds that are usually loud ones—
VERY VERY LOUD?
Can you make the sounds that are usually soft sounds—
very
very
soft?

799. What work do people do? Can you dance the work done by:

your mother?   your father?
the carpenter?   the doctor?
the truck driver?   the violinist?
the cashier at the supermarket?

Can you dance a person who doesn't have a job?

800. Can you dance a rocking horse
        or
a horse on the merry-go-round?

801. Rub-a-dub-dub on a washboard with a stick,
   a nail,
         or
   your fingernail.

802. Have you ever blown across the tip of an empty bottle?
   When you put water in the bottle, does it sound the
   same?

803. Did you ever listen to music that had a kind of "smooth"
   feeling?
   What about a rough feeling? a stiffish feeling? a soft
   fluffy feeling like clouds?
   Can you choose a feeling and dance to it?

804. Is your friend leaving? Wave good-bye with a dance.
   Can you finger-wave good-bye with a dance too?

805. Dance a yo-yo!

806. Can you hiss? buzz?
   Can you blow through your teeth?

807. Are you able to sit absolutely quiet and not move a mus-
   cle when you listen to a fast polka?

808. Does yellow make you feel light and merry? Dance yel-
   low.
   Dance red.
   Dance black.

809. Can you dance a grandfather clock, swaying back and
   forth to the ticking?

810. Are there any places where you can't sing?

811. Can you dance a rag doll?
     (It really isn't lazy even though it feels so-o-o limp.)

812. Sing and dance a weeping willow tree.

813. Can you dance an octopus?

814. How many different sounds can you make with a walnut shell?

815. Did you ever dance with a broomstick?

816. Can you dance like a butterfly that is caught in a net?

817. Can you dance as though you were jelly?

818. Can you dance a typewriter?

819. Can you make up and sing a song beginning "I wish I were _____"?

820. Dance being freezing cold.
     Dance being so-o-o hot and tired.

821. Don't peek—but can you tell with your eyes closed if someone is

     hopping?
     skipping?
     sliding?   or

jumping?

822. Did you ever notice how feather-light deer seem as they leap and run?
Dance a deer!

823. Is there a cut-up piece of an old garden hose you can have?
Hum into it.
Hum into one end of it and listen to what comes out the other end!

824. How would you dance if you were an ice-cream cone and started melting
and melting
till there was only a puddle on the floor?

825. Don't let anyone correct you when you dance.
If you feel like whirling—then whirl.
Do you want to gallop? skip? hop? stretch? jump? swing? bounce? twist?
Do you feel like dancing tip-toe?

826. Can you tap the rhythm of the names of your friends?
For example:
E-liz-a-beth
Pa-tri-cia
Jen-ni-fer
Jon-a-than

827. Tap out "Row, Row, Row Your Boat" and see who can guess what the song is. Do another song. What about "Three Blind Mice"?

828. Can you dance as if you were so very sad inside and your heart just ached?
Now dance a little more quickly and look up.
Are you happier?
How wonderful I feel!

829. Can you make your voice sound like a bee? whistle like a bird?
Can you make a block of wood patter?
What sound does a wire brush make?
If you crushed cellophane, would it sound like fire crackling?

830. Can you make up a song about your new shoes?
Are they stiff?
Are they slippery?
Do they hurt sometimes?
Do you like your new shoes?

831. Dance "Jack in the Box."
How crowded he is in that box.
Wouldn't he just love to get out!
He did! Wheeeeeee!

832. Can you sing your name loud.
Can you sing your name soft,
and softer,
and softer,
and softer,
till
you
can't hear it anymore?

833. Do all clocks sound the same?
Did you ever hear a town clock say "ding"?
a grandfather clock say "dong"?   or

the kitchen clock say "tic-a-tock"?
Can you dance the grandfather clock at midnight?

834. Have you ever played a musical "Follow the Leader" game?

    First, you sing a song and decide how you want to move.

    Then everyone sings and moves like you.

    Try it! It's a lot of fun!

835. If your mother sings just one sound or plays one note on a piano—could you make a sound that is just like her sound?

836. Pour water into a glass until it is full.

    Pour water into another glass until it is half-full.

    Strike each glass with a pencil.

    Listen to the sound each glass makes.

    Do you hear one glass make a HIGH sound? which one?

    Do you hear one glass make a LOW sound? which one?

837. Do you have a recording of Vivaldi's "Four Seasons"?
Play it and dance:

being seeds	sprouting
growing	waving in the breeze
being rained on	forming buds

838. Can you walk and dance:

like your grandfather?
like your mom and dad?
bumpy like a cowboy?

the way baby walks?
jerky like a robot?
like Henny Penny?

839. Can you swing your arms like:

a railroad signal?
a propeller?

a clock pendulum?
a cow's tail?

840. Everyone will enjoy a "bell tree" you can make from a branch of a tree mounted in a heavy block and decorated with different bells.
Wouldn't that make a very special gift for someone you love?

841. Walk in time to music, but when it stops—you must squat.
Then go on and walk when the music plays again.
Instead of squatting, change it to:

freezing
jumping
or just standing still.

bouncing
hopping

842. Try saying "You're the most terrible, terrible dog in the world" to your dog in a warm, loving way
and
see the way
he will wag his tail!

843. Listen to Handel's "Water Music," and draw a picture of what the music makes you feel like drawing.

844. If someone claps once, you clap once, too. If someone claps three times, you clap three times too.
If someone claps like this: C L A P, clap, clap—can you do that too?

If someone claps like this: clap, clap, C L A P—can you do that?

What other ways can you change the clapping?

845. When you strike a triangle softly, does it make a sound like:

a little baby's feet?
a tinkle bell?

Can you make the triangle sound like:

a train bell?
a storm?
a fire engine bell?
the ice-cream truck bell?

Can you make the triangle sound like a hammer on a rock?

846. Most of us walk straight ahead. But do you know that there are other ways to walk? Try these ways:

Walk with your feet turned out.
Walk with them turned in.
Walk stepping high.
Walk stepping low.
Walk on your toes.
Walk on your heels.
Can you crunch your heels?

847. Mark, Steven, and Malaika are good examples of names that have these rhythms:

jump (Mark)
walk (Steven)
skip (Malaika)

Say the names and clap as you say them
or
tap the tabletop to them.

INSTRUMENTS

No home with a young child should be without a drawerful of some of the homemade instruments always ready for instant use.

If you decide to have a marching band go around the block

or

if there is going to be a backyard birthday party,

it is very important that the leader and members of the band wear special hats. These can be brown paper bags with the edges rolled back.

Also, if someone wishes to play an instrument solo, it is just fine to play without accompaniment. However, if accompaniment is required, try the radio or a record. The very best accompaniment is to sing a song you know.

848. *Pot-Cover Cymbals*

Dance away to the clang of two flat pot lids when they are banged together. Can you make loud and soft sounds?

849. *Xylophone*

Put different amounts of water into drinking glasses or pop bottles and tap them with a spoon. Hear the different sounds they make. They will sound like bells ringing just for you.

850. *Rattles*

Some dried beans or pebbles in a tin can will make an elegant rattle. Or try bottle caps on a string.

Dried beans between two stapled paper plates are good too.

MUSIC AND RHYTHM WONDERS

851. *Rhythm Sticks*

When you tap two sticks together, you have a set of
rhythm sticks.
(Of course, if you attach ribbon streamers to them, they
become quite glamorous.)

852. *Violin or Guitar*

Take the cover off a small wooden box (a cigar box is
good, if you can find one) and stretch rubber bands
across it. If the rubber bands have different thick-
nesses, they will make different sounds. (For example, a thick rubber band will make low notes.)
Then just pluck away.

853. *"Poor Man's Harmonica"*

Have you ever heard of the "Poor Man's Harmonica"?
All it is, is an old-fashioned hair comb covered with
tissue paper. Then all you need to do is to sing or
hum on it with your mouth slightly open. (It tickles
just a little bit.)

854. *Drum or Tom-tom*

Any one of these things would make a fine drum for
any marching band.
Listen and you will hear that each of them makes a different sound.
Which would you choose?

a kitchen pot or pan
a metal or plastic pail
a plastic bleach bottle
any big can, such as a coffee or paint can
any empty oatmeal box

855. *Chimes*

> Get a stick or a ruler, dangle a knife, a fork, and a tea-spoon from one end of it, and tap it with a spoon. What a glorious set of chimes you have!

856. *Potato Grater*

> If you have a potato grater, you can get four different sounds, one from each side. Do you know how?

LEARNING SONGS

> Here are some fun ways to learn lots of important things (parents will be glad to help).

> For example, here is a way to learn your telephone number:

857. Do you know the tune of "Twinkle, Twinkle, Little Star"? Change the words of the song to the numbers of your telephone number.
Now sing the song over and over again, saying the numbers instead of the words.

> Even if you think you can't sing, sing it anyway.
> Sing it when you do the dishes; when you take a shower; in the car; when you take a walk.

TWINKLE, TWINKLE LITTLE STAR (familiar tune)

Twin-kle, twin-kle, lit-tle star.
  8   7   6   4   8 7   2

How I won-der what you are.
  8 7 6   4   8   7 2

Up a-bove the world so high,
  8 7 6   4   8   7   2

Like a dia-mond in the sky.
  8 7 6   4   8 7   2

Twin-kle, twin-kle, lit-tle star,
  8   7   6   4 8 7   2

How I won-der what you are.
  8 7 6   4   8   7   2

Objective: To learn your telephone number.

858. MUFFIN MAN (familiar tune)

What do you do when the light is red?
light is red?
light is red?
What do you do when the light is red?
I stop, stop, stop, stop, stop.

Continue on with "What do you do when the light is green?" (go)
"What do you do when the light is yellow?" (yield)

Objective: To learn the meaning of traffic light colors.

859. LONDON BRIDGE IS FALLING DOWN (familiar tune)

Tell me how the kitten talks
kitten talks
kitten talks
Tell me how the kitten talks
Me oo, me oo, me oo, me oo.

Continue with the doggy (bow wow)
the cow (moo moo)
sheep (baa baa)
duck (quack quack)
etc.

Objective: To learn the sounds of animals.

860. MARY HAD A LITTLE LAMB (familiar tune)

Mary Jones is my name
is my name
is my name
Mary Jones is my name
Mary is my name.

Continue with sister's and brother's names, parents'
names, friend's name, and so on.

Objective: To learn one's name and others' names.

861. THE ALPHABET OR ABC SONG (familiar tune)

A B C D E F G H I J K L M N O P Q R S T U V W X Y Z
Now I know my ABCs,
Next time won't you sing with me?

862. FRERE JACQUES (familiar tune)

Raise your right hand
Raise your right hand
Your right hand
Your right hand
Raise your right hand higher
Raise your right hand higher
Right, right, right
Right, right, right.

Continue on with left hand, right and left foot, and so on.

Objective: To learn to identify right and left hands and feet.

863. ROW, ROW, ROW YOUR BOAT (familiar tune)

Touch, touch, touch your nose.
Touch your nose this way.
Touch, touch, touch your nose.
Touch your nose this way.

Continue on with ears, eyes, arms, knees, toes, and so on, touching each body part as it is named.

Objective: To learn parts of the body.

864. YANKEE DOODLE (familiar tune)

I'm walking, walking, walking, walking
Walking, walking, walking.
I'm walking, walking, walking, walking
Walking, walking, walking.

Change action to running, jumping, skipping, hopping, and so on.

Objective: To learn to name various physical movements.

865. HAPPY BIRTHDAY TO YOU (familiar tune)

How old am I?
How old am I?
How old am I?
How old am I?

I'm _____ years old.
I'm _____ years old.
I'm _____ years old.
I'm _____ years old.

(Raise the same number of fingers as age is given.)

Objective: To learn one's age.

866. GO TELL AUNT RHODY (familiar tune)

I've got a penny.
I've got a penny.
I've got a penny.
One, one, one, one, one, one.

Continue with two, three, four and five pennies, holding up the proper amount each time.

Continue with a nickel, dime, and quarter—holding up one of them each time.

Objective: To learn to count to five.

867. THE FARMER IN THE DELL (familiar tune)

In the morning I wake up.
In the morning I wake up.
In the morning I wake up.
In the morning I wake up.

Continue with "Then I brush my teeth."
"Then I make my bed."
"Then I put my play clothes on."
"Then I eat my breakfast."

Act out each activity.

Objective: To learn about daily routine.

868. GO ROUND AND ROUND THE VILLAGE (familiar tune)

(Suggestion: Fit action to words.)

Let's walk around the table.
Let's walk around the table.

Let's walk around the table.
Let's walk and walk and walk.

Continue with jump, skip, hop, march, gallop, run, tiptoe.
Demonstrate each action word.

Objective: To learn the meaning of "action" words.

869. JINGLE BELLS (familiar tune)

1 2 3
4 5 6
7 8 9 and 10

1 2 3
4 5 6
7 8 9 and 10

(Raise a finger as each number is given.)

Objective: To learn to count to ten.

870. DID YOU EVER SEE A LASSIE? (familiar tune)

I can play a horn.
I can play a horn.
I can play a horn.
Toot, toot, toot, toot, toot.

Continue with drum (boom, boom),
violin (hm, hm),
trumpet (toot, toot).

Play the instrument as each is sung.

Objective: To become familiar with musical instruments and their sounds.

871. GOOD MORNING TO YOU (familiar tune)

Good morning to you.

Good morning to you.
Good morning to you.
Good morning to you.

Continue with "Good afternoon," "Good evening," "Thank you so much," and so forth.

Objective: To learn common terms of courtesy.

PRESCHOOL WONDERS

"If you want me to learn . . . please don't hurry me . . .
Let me play around with the things you have for me . . .
Let me find out things for myself . . .
I just know I can learn lots of things . . .
. . . in time . . .
. . . if you don't hurry me. . . ."

(Have you ever thought this to yourself?)

872. Can you finish what these say?

I feel happy when _____.
I feel sad when _____.
I'm scared when _____.
I get so excited when _____.
I like to be by myself when _____.

873. Can you make up a short poem with words that rhyme?
(They can be as silly as you like.)

I saw a man.   There was a fish.
He ate a pan.   It lived in a dish.

A tiny snail   The old tree
crawled out of my pail.   is the home of the bee.

874. Is there anything more fun than to snuggle up on the
sofa with a parent or to "read" a favorite story together
before going to bed?

875. Talk about the birthday party you went to, or:

the dream you had

the movie you saw
the book you "read"
what you did on the weekend
the accident you saw
the baby bird on the sidewalk

876. What are some things that go UP and DOWN?

birds?   elevators?   what else?

877. Do you know "Twinkle, Twinkle Little Star"? Can you sing it LOUD? Can you sing it in a SOFT voice?

Do you have a radio? Can you play it LOUD? Can you play it SOFT?

If you put some pebbles in a jar—could you shake them so they would make a LOUD sound? a SOFT sound?

Can you close your book with a SOFT sound? (Never close a book with a LOUD sound!)

878. How many words can you think of that begin with the sound:

mmmmmmmmmm?   dddddddddd?
rrrrrrrrrr?   bbbbbbbbbb?

879. How many times can you bounce a ball?

880. Make a map of your street. Make little boxes for the houses—and, if you can find and put the house numbers in the boxes, it would be a very fine map.

If you have a mailbox or a fire hydrant at the corner, put those in too. Does your neighborhood have a post office, corner drugstore, grocery store, library? Add those too!

881. Do you know the "days of the week"?
Do you know what day today is?
what day yesterday was?
what day it will be tomorrow?
your birthday?

882. If the lids were taken off your pots and pans, would you be able to match each pot and pan with its own lid?

883. How many trucks can you spot in a ten-minute ride in the car?

884. Walk around your block and count:

dogs   joggers
white houses   churches
brick houses   people riding their bicycles

885. Sit quietly on the porch. How many birds do you see?

886. Trace a penny and try to copy the picture on it. Do you see the date on the penny? (The date tells you when the penny was made.) Can you read the numbers on the date?

887. Go through your books, magazines, and newspapers to find pictures of words that begin with a "B" sound—or any other sound in the alphabet. Can you make an ALPHABET BOOK with different letters you cut out? Can you "write" your name with the letters?

888. Look through your house and find things that come in the shape of a circle. Such as:

the clock   saucers
the fan   a roll of plastic tape

889. Do you have a "family time" at your home?
It's a good time to take part in conversations like:

What I think about . . .
What I did today . . .
How the garden is doing . . .
Some special news events . . .
The peace demonstration . . .

890. You can have all kinds of "treasure hunts" in your house.
For example:

for straight things	for high things	for dark things
for curved things	for low things	for sharp things

891. Just think—what would it be like if:

houses had no windows?	every day were Sunday?
dogs didn't bark?	we didn't have friends?

892. Do you know the OPPOSITE GAME? Someone says one word and you think of the opposite word, a word that is altogether different. Here are some to try out:

fat (thin)	old (new)	full (empty)
quiet (noisy)	up (down)	dry (wet)
hard (soft)	fast (slow)	straight (crooked)

Can you think of any others?

893. Can you print your name with chalk?

with bottle caps?	with nuts?
with stones?	with a twig—on soil?

894. How many beds are in your home?
Who has the biggest bed? the middle-sized bed? the smallest?
What else comes in different sizes?

895. Get out one pair of shoes for each member of the family and see if you can line them up from the *smallest* to the BIGGEST.

What else can you line up from the *smallest* to the BIGGEST?

896. "Type" a letter to Grandpa or a friend on a typewriter. (Typing with one finger is just fine and so is any "made-up spelling.")

897. Name some things you can put ON and OFF:

your pants?   the faucet?   your eyeglasses?
the lights?   the radio?   what else?

898. Next time you eat an apple, count the number of seeds it has.

899. If your parents will allow it, can you make a "family tree" with photographs?

Begin with your grandparents   OR
if you are lucky enough to have your great grandparents—that would be even better!

900. How well can you follow one instruction? Such as:

"Bring me the book."   "Sit down."
"Close the door."   "Stand up."

Now, see how well you can follow two instructions:

"Bring me the book and sit down."
"Close the door and open the window."
"Sit down and draw a picture."

901. When you see a red fire hydrant, a red fire engine, or a red traffic light—does "red" tell you something?

What are some things that are green? What does the "green" tell you?

What about yellow?

902. You can start learning how to "look" when you keep a diary about your pet. For example:

June 2 19__   We bought Squeaky at the pet shop.
               Squeaky has a long tail.
               I like Squeaky a lot.
June 4 19__   Squeaky fell off the table.
               Mother found her in Dad's shoe.
               We put Squeaky back in her cage.
June 9 19__   Squeaky had seven babies.
               They are so cute. I wish I could hold them.
               I love them a lot.

903. You can make some silly pictures if you mix up parts like this:

Find a picture of (for example) an automobile that has a driver at the wheel.

Cut out the driver, paste in a picture of a dog's head instead—and then try to keep from laughing!

Can you think of some other silly pictures you can make?

904. How many of these SIGNS have you seen? Do you know what they mean?

STOP	RESTROOM	EXIT
GO	MEN	QUIET
DANGER	WOMEN	BOYS
KEEP OFF THE GRASS	GIRLS	BUS STOP

905. Do you know your first name? and your last name?

your address?   the city you live in?
the state you live in?   your telephone number?
how old you are?   your birthday?

906. Here are some fun books any child can make. Or perhaps making a collage would be more fun?

THINGS I LIKE TO DO

THINGS I DON'T LIKE TO DO

HAPPINESS IS _____

HOW I COULD HELP OTHER PEOPLE

THINGS I LIKE TO DO WITH MOTHER

THINGS I LIKE TO DO WITH FATHER

THINGS I LIKE TO DO AT GRANDMA'S HOUSE

THINGS I LIKE TO DO WITH EVERYONE IN THE FAMILY

FOOD I LIKE TO EAT

PLACES I WOULD LIKE TO GO TO

WHAT I WOULD LIKE TO BE SOMEDAY

PEOPLE WHO HELP ME

HOUSES THAT OTHER PEOPLE LIVE IN

907. How many steps go from the first floor of your house to the bedroom on the second floor?
How many steps are there going up to the attic?
How many steps are at the front entrance to your house?
How many steps are there at the back of your house?

908. How many buttons are on your sweater?
Do you have buttons on your snowsuit? your raincoat? your sweaters? shirts?

909. If you have a yogurt or cottage cheese carton (with a lid), cut a little slit in the lid. Now you have an excellent bank for saving pennies.

Do you have a penny in your pocket for your bank?

Count the money you have in the bank from time to time.

910. Get a box and an object (acorn, stone, etc.). Place the object:

on the box	*beside* the box	*in* the box
under the box	*outside* the box	*over* the box

911. What are some things that always seem to go together?

salt and pepper	pots and pans
Jack and Jill	shoes and socks

What else?

912. "Read" the newspapers with your parents.

Find photographs you may wish to discuss.

Go over the weather forecast, advertisements, local events, health columns, lost and found.

Find the cartoons and see if you can understand them.

Do you have a favorite comic strip?

913. Look about your house. Do you see anything made from rubber? (Any rubber balls, heels on shoes, erasers?)

What things can you find that are made from wood? glass? plastic? metal? leather?

914. What are three ways to show that you:

like your new neighbor?	love your father?
like your new dress?	like the apple pie?
are sorry your friend is sick?	like the sunshine?

915. Did you ever play the "Observation Game"? All you need to do is:

> Put three objects on the table. Look carefully at them.
> Close your eyes while one object is taken away.
> Open your eyes. Do you know what is missing?
> Someday play this game with five different objects.

916. When you go for a walk, find the street numbers of the houses you pass. Can you read what the numbers are?

917. You can learn lots of new things if you ask "why."

> Why do we see so many worms after a rain?
> Why do bears sleep all winter?
> Why do people cry? why do they laugh?
> Why do leaves fall from trees?
> Why do flowers die?

918. Clip off the heads, feet, and tails of animals in pictures— and mix them up. Can you put them back together again the way they were?

> (You can make some awfully strange-looking animals if you don't match them up right!)

919. If the lids were taken off your pots and pans, would you be able to match each pot and pan with its own lid?

920. Can you rearrange these words to make short sentences?

like you I	kitten purr hear I the
pretty is flower the	bike red my is
cookie good is my	fast truck goes the

Can you make up some of your own?

921. How many worms can you see when you turn over some earth in the garden?

922. Comparisons:

Walking in dry leaves sounds like _____.
The wind sounds like _____.
Ice cream tastes like _____.
Snow looks like _____.

923. What are three nice things you can say about your:

mother?   sister or brother?
father?   friend?

924. Can you make up your own riddle using three clues? For example:

What is long, thin, and you write with it?
What is made of wood, has four legs, and you eat on it?

Make up some other ones.

925. Can you talk a little bit about:

the rainstorm you had last night?   your stomachache?
a radio program you liked?   the eggs that hatched?

926. Can you finish these?

Ice cream and cake usually mean _____.
Cats and dogs usually mean _____.
Sneezes, runny nose, and fever usually mean _____.
Lions, monkeys, and giraffes usually mean _____.

927. Many people of the community are health-and-safety helpers. Do you know who they are?

Who gives you health checkups and vaccinations?
Who cleans the streets and collects the garbage?
Who keeps stray animals from running around loose?
Who makes sure that people obey traffic rules?
Who checks your teeth and gums?
Who puts out fires?

928. Wouldn't you love to have an "alone" place where you could just be by yourself?

> See if you can make one with a great big cardboard carton and cut out a hole so you can get into it.
>
> Can you go behind the furniture and have a little collection of books to "read"?
>
> Would you be able to have part of a rug just for yourself?
>
> Is there an "unbusy" part of the house? Perhaps just a corner would do.
>
> If you drape sheets over a couch, you have a tent.

929. Sometime—over the dinner table—would you like everyone to discuss:

> What would happen if _____?
> How can we be sure that _____?
> What was it like when _____?
> What will it be like when _____?

930. Can you change the ending of some of your favorite fairy tales? Try these:

> Snow White   Hansel and Gretel
> Cinderella   Little Red Riding Hood
> Beauty and the Beast Rumpelstiltskin

931. What are some things that come in:

> ONE'S   (your nose, you, horn on unicorn)
>
> TWO'S   (eyes, twins, feet)
>
> THREE'S   (tricycle wheels, triplets)
>
> FOUR'S   (wheels on a car, four-leaf clover)
>
> FIVE'S   (fingers, toes)

932. If you create a "Family Newspaper" you could be the editor-in-chief. Relatives who live far away would be glad to get a copy of it from time to time.

It could include drawings of news items such as:

the new kitten	sports events	family visits
a tooth that came out	graduations	weddings

933. If you had a mixed-up collection of different colored socks, could you sort them into the different colors (red, blue, green, white, etc.)?

Could you sort them into different sizes? (big ones, little ones, babies)?

Collect knives (not sharp ones), forks, and spoons, and then see if you can sort them out into piles.

934. Have a library right in your own home or backyard. You could collect books, comics, magazines, records, and so forth and lend them out to the neighborhood children.

935. What is the very first thing that comes to mind when you hear these words:

dentist	kangaroo	peanut butter
ice cubes	lightning	elf
comb	kitten	butter
worms	canary	thunder
frog	parakeet	tiger

936. Find things in your kitchen that are round. Do you see:

a water glass?	a bowl?
a plate?	what else?

Find things that are square. Do you see:

a napkin?	a slice of bread?

Find things that come in triangles. Do you have:

a piece of pie?	a slice of pizza?

937. If your wishes could all come true, what would you wish for the most?

938. Make up a story that took place:

at a picnic	at the zoo	at the play yard
in a rainstorm	on the moon	in the attic

939. Can you make up an animal riddle? Such as:

I eat grass.
I say moo.
What am I?

Can you make up a fruit riddle? Such as:

I'm red inside.	You eat me sliced.
I'm juicy.	What am I?

940. Can you talk about "YOU"?

My name is . . .	I like to . . .
I live at . . .	I look forward to . . .
My friends are . . .	I get angry when . . .
I am happiest when . . .	I feel proud when . . .
You should see my . . .	When I was little . . .
My mother is . . .	I want to be . . .
My father is . . .	I like stories when . . .
My favorite things are . . .	I feel afraid when . . .
I just love . . .	

941. Your whole house and all the outdoors are made-to-order for COLOR WALKS.

Keep your eyes wide open and you'll see more colors than you ever thought there would be.

Start with one color and search all over for things that are that one color. Can you find three things? five? more?

942. Can you count the petals on the daisy?

Can you write your name with raisins or bottle caps? nuts or stones?

943. Take a one-block walk and count how many of these things you see:

How many houses are there? trees? street lights? children?

Do you see a rabbit?

Are any buses picking up children for school?

Do you see any baby carriages?

944. See if you can make up a sentence with three words that rhyme. (Your sentences can be as silly as you like.) Here are some to begin with:

tree, bee, see   draw, paw, straw

bake, cake, lake   tail, snail, mail

945. Talk about: what you want to be "when I grow up"
the time you got lost
"what I did today"

946. When you go riding on a bus or a subway with your parents, keep your eyes open to see:

how the fares are paid

how you get transfers

how you get change

how you get tokens

how to let the conductor know when you have to "get off"

Would you be able to do this yourself someday when you are older?

947. Make a "Me" Book containing: my fingerprints
my hair
my handprint
a photograph of me

TONGUE TWISTERS

Try to say each tongue twister five times.
Try to say it faster
and faster!

948. A big blue bucket of blue blueberries.

949. Ten tiny ticks throwing terrible temper tantrums.

950. Beautiful babbling brooks bubble between blossoming banks.

951. She sells seashells by the seashore.

952. Peter Piper picked a peck of pickled peppers;
A peck of pickled peppers Peter Piper picked.
If Peter Piper picked a peck of pickled peppers,
Where's the peck of pickled peppers Peter Piper picked?

953. How much dew could a dewdrop drop if a dewdrop could drop dew?

954. Susan shines shoes and socks.
Shoes and socks shines Susan.

955. Six thick thistle sticks.

956. Three gray geese sat on the green grass grazing.

957. A man with a duster made a furious bluster
Dusting a bust in the hall.
When the bust, it was dusted,
The bust it was busted.
The bust, it was dust—
That is all!

958. Whether the weather be fine,
Or whether the weather be not,
Whether the weather be cold
Or whether the weather be hot,
We'll weather the weather,
Whatever the weather,
Whether we like it or not.

959. Sheep shouldn't sleep in a shack.
Sheep should sleep in a shed.

960. A noise annoys an oyster,
but a noisy noise annoys an oyster more.

961. A big black bug bit a big black bear.

962. Betty Botter bought some butter.
"But," she said,
"This butter's bitter.
If I put it in my batter,
It will make the batter bitter."
So Betty bought some better butter,

better than the bitter butter,
and she put it in the batter,
and it made the batter better.

963. Round and round the rough and ragged rock the ragged rascal ran.

964. The swan swam out to the sea; swim, swan, swim!

RIDDLES

Here's a riddle:

When you first hear me, I seem so hard to figure out.
When someone tells you the answer, it just seems so simple.
What am I? (Answer: a riddle!)

In riddles, words are played around with and the answers seem like nonsense. But you don't seem to mind being fooled. In fact—it's lots of fun! Besides, don't riddles make you think a bit too?

965. What's the hardest thing about learning to skate?
The ice.

966. When is a boy most like a bear?
When he's barefoot.

967. What is the easiest thing to part with?
A comb.

968. How can your pocket be empty and still have something in it?
It can have a hole in it.

969. When do elephants have eight feet?

When there are two of them.

970. Would you rather have a lion chase you or a gorilla?

I'd rather have him chase the gorilla.

971. What's worse than a worm in an apple?

Half a worm.

972. What did one carrot say to the other carrot?

Nothing. Carrots can't talk.

973. What is over your head and under your hat?

Your hair.

974. What can go through the water and yet never gets wet?

Sunlight.

975. What did the floor say to the wall?

I'll meet you at the corner.

976. Why do birds like to fly south for the winter?

Because it's too far to walk.

977. What is taller sitting than standing?

A dog.

978. It acts like a cat, looks like a cat, yet it isn't a cat. What is it?

A kitten.

979. What is it that belongs to you, but others use it more than you do?

Your name.

980. Why are fish so smart?

Because they go around in schools.

981. What must a stork do to stand on one foot?

Hold up the other foot.

982. What's the strongest animal you know?

A snail, because it carries its house on its back.

983. What always goes up when the rain comes down?

An umbrella.

984. Three women went walking under one umbrella, but none of them got wet. Why?

IT WASN'T RAINING.

IDIOMS

Nobody knows where idioms came from, but people use them every day. An idiom is a group of words that don't mean what they literally say. They say one thing but mean something a little different. Here are some:

985. As scarce as hen's teeth

Something that is hard to find. Hens don't even have teeth.

986. A "green thumb"

A person who loves to work in gardens and knows what to do to make plants grow well.

987. Fish out of water

Something that isn't really where it belongs.

988. Walking on thin ice
   Doing something that is dangerous.

989. A person who is "all eyes"
   Someone who sees everything and watches very care-
      fully.

990. Button your lip
   Close your mouth or stop talking.

991. Someone who is "all ears"
   Someone who is listening very carefully.

PROVERBS

A *proverb* is something generally very wise and quite
true. The Bible even devotes a book to proverbs. You
often hear them in peoples' conversations. Some are
simple enough to discuss with children at the dinner
table. Try these:

992. The apple doesn't fall far from the tree.
   Great oaks from little acorns grow.
   Don't put all your eggs in one basket.

AESOP'S FABLES

Do you know that *Aesop's Fables* have been around
since 620 B.C.! How many millions of children have
enjoyed hearing them and thinking about the truisms
that have existed through the centuries! You can read
and discuss these with your child today too.

993. THE MILKMAID AND HER PAIL

The milkmaid was going to market carrying her milk in a pail on her head. As she went along she began deciding what she would do with the money she would get for the milk. "I'll buy some fowls from Farmer Brown," she said, "and they will lay eggs each morning, which I will sell to the parson's wife. With the money that I get from the sale of these eggs, I will buy myself a new dress and a hat; and when I go to market, won't all the young men come up and speak to me! My friends will be jealous; but I don't care. I shall just look at them and toss my head like this." As she spoke, she tossed her head back, the pail fell off, and all the milk was spilt. So she had to go home and tell her mother what had happened.

"Ah, my child," said her mother, "do not count the chickens before they are hatched."

994. THE SHEPHERD BOY AND THE WOLF

A mischievous lad, who was sent to mind some sheep, in jest used to cry "Wolf! Wolf!" When the people at work in the neighboring fields came running to the spot, he would laugh at them for their pains. One day a wolf came in reality, and this time, the boy called "Wolf! Wolf!" in earnest; but the men, having been so often deceived, disregarded his cries, and the sheep were left at the mercy of the wolf.

995. THE GREEDY DOG

A dog stole a bone and ran away with it in his jaws. Soon he came to a stream. He started to cross it on a fallen log. As he walked, he stared down into the water. There he saw another dog with another bone.

He paused. "His bone is bigger than mine," he thought.

He snapped at it. As he did, his own bone fell into the water.

"My bone is gone," said the dog, "because I was too greedy."

996. THE MICE AND THE CAT

A cat was very quiet and very quick. She killed lots of mice. One day the mice got together. "What can we do?" asked the leader. "Each of us must think of a plan. The one with the best plan wins some cheese."

One of the mice spoke up. "Let's tie a bell to the cat's neck," he said. "If we hear her coming, we can get away."

His plan was cheered by most of the mice. "Do I get the cheese?" he asked.

"No," said the leader. "While we are trying to tie on the bell, the cat will eat us."

997. THE WOLF IN SHEEP'S CLOTHING

A wolf wrapped himself in the skin of a sheep and got into a sheep pen. He ate a lamb, but at last the shepherd found him.

"Don't throw me out," said the wolf. "I'm one of your sheep."

"No," said the shepherd. "You're only pretending to be a sheep. I know you are really a wolf."

"How do you know?" asked the wolf. "I look like a sheep."

"Yes," said the shepherd. "But you act like a wolf." He beat the wolf with a stick and drove him away.

998. THE CROW AND THE PITCHER

A thirsty crow came to a pitcher of water. She was sad to find that she wasn't able to drink. The water was too low. Her beak could not reach it. She sat on some pebbles in a ditch to think.

At last she lifted a pebble in her beak and dropped it into the pitcher. Then she dropped another and another. The water rose higher and higher. At last it reached the top, and the thirsty crow drank her fill.

POETRY

How children love *poetry*—its rhyme, rhythm, the stories and thoughts, and its nonsense too. They love the same poems over and over and over again. They might even like to sing them, chant them, and get to know them by heart. If a child hears poetry in early childhood, the child may soon want to write his or her own poetry. You'll help with the writing and spelling of course!

999. WHERE GO THE BOATS?

Dark brown is the river,
    Golden is the sand.
It flows along for ever,
    With trees on either hand.

Green leaves a-floating,
    Castles of the foam,
Boats of mine a-boating—
    Where will all come home?
        —*Robert Louis Stevenson*

1000. WHO HAS SEEN THE WIND?

Who has seen the wind?
    Neither I nor you:
But when the leaves hang trembling,
    The wind is passing through.

Who has seen the wind?
    Neither you nor I:
But when the trees bow down their heads,
    The wind is passing by.
                    —Christina Rossetti

1001. THE SWING

How do you like to go up in a swing,
    Up in the air so blue?
Oh, I do think it the pleasantest thing
    Ever a child can do!

Up in the air and over the wall,
    Till I can see so wide,
Rivers and trees and cattle and all
    Over the countryside—

Till I look down on the garden green,
    Down on the roof so brown—
Up in the air I go flying again,
    Up in the air and down!
                  —Robert Louis Stevenson